PAPER

GRADERS

NOTES FROM

THE ACADEMIC UNDERCLASS

EDITED BY

BARRY ROBERTS GREER

First published on computer disk in 1994 by the Cairn Press of Oregon.

ISBN-13: 978-1479185375
ISBN-10: 147918537X

CONTENTS

Judy Wells

If the men and women who tell their stories in *Paper Graders: Notes from the Academic Underclass* were doing something of no importance, they could hardly be treated more carelessly, and even contemptuously, than they are in many U.S. schools of higher education. These "paper graders" or "migrant workers" or "academic gypsies" or "comp dogs" are teachers who are not on the tenure track. They struggle along on salaries that are a fraction of what their more privileged colleagues make. Many have no benefits or job security or even a desk where they can stow their grade book. "Yo-yo teachers," as one of the writers in this volume calls them, they can be engaged at short notice and let go without warning. And yet they teach courses that everyone believes are basic to a good education.

But unlike many exploited workers, these comp dogs are not mute. They write poems and essays and stories about the injustice of their situation. They are understandably. angry; they are also eloquent. This book gives us a chance to hear what they have to say. Many people will be surprised at the ugly realities behind the humane facade of many colleges and universities. This book is for them.

Albert Shanker
Washington, D.C.

INTRODUCTION

Usually revelations of corruption in general and labor exploitation in particular are written by former professors sitting a safe distance from campus· with an independent income, professors such as historian Page Smith, author of *Killing the Spirit: Higher Education in America.* Smith mentions in his history of the rise and demise of the American university that "Lately the university has . . . an increasing dependence on 'lecturers,' heavily concentrated in the areas of language instruction and remedial English. They are denied the lofty title of professor, paid less, required to teach many more hours since they are not expected [and don't have the time] to publish books and articles; they are the peons of the academic world, second-class citizens in a supposedly democratic community of scholars" (119). Or by journalists such as Charles Sykes, who also mentions "the peons of the academic world" in passing in *Profscam* and *The Hollow Men* on his reactionary muckraking way to excoriating and exorcising the liberal PC crowd now in power on the late twentieth-century American campus.

It is rare, though, to read notes from the underclass, the peons, the second-class citizens. Those who do speak up take the risk I took when I published "Educating Joshua" in 1989, an essay about teaching the Oregon governor's son in the corrupt Oregon State University English Department. The risk I took publishing "Comp Dog," a profile of a used and abused English instructor printed as a sidebar in 1990 for "Paper Graders," an expose of labor exploitation and union busting at the University of Oregon. And in 1993, two years after my exile began, I published "The Only Good Writer is a Dead Writer."

It took two years because the Greers had to scramble to survive after Barry lost his job. We rise from stubborn Highland lineage and we did survive, and I did find the time to write "Good Writer," an essay that explained why I blew the whistle and chronicles OSU's 1989-1991 effort to punish me for blowing that whistle louder than the power boys and girls liked. "Good Writer" found 75,000 readers in March of 1993, as the third in a front-page censorship series published by *Writer's N.W.,* a trade paper for the Northwest's literary community. *WNW* had a thousand word limit, so I've used the anthology as an excuse to print the entire text and to solicit and publish prose and poetry from Alaska to California to Colorado to New Jersey to clearly demonstrate that labor exploitation in higher education is the rule, not the exception. And that knowledge, I hope, will lead others in the underclass to understand, at minimum, that they are not the cause of their condition.

The first three essays in the anthology serve as a general introduction to the causes and consequences of those second-class working conditions. David Ehrenfeld offers one of the best short overviews I've read on why an academic underclass was created and is growing in number. M. Elizabeth Wallace offers a detailed analysis of life in the underclass in Oregon public higher education, an essay followed by "Paper Graders," or life in the underclass at the University of Oregon, a typical tax-supported state higher education institution.

After the introduction, the anthology moves your attention to the voices of people who survive in the underclass day to day, term to term, semester to semester. These are the voices of poets and writers who know well the fear, anger, and absurdity of teaching "in a supposedly democratic community of scholars." They know the fear of ending up like Greer for speaking up about their working conditions. They know the anger of being used and abused and having no power to stop it. They know the absurdity of academic freedom in a system where they teach what they cannot honestly practice--open inquiry, critical thinking, and the free expression of that thinking.

There is no doubt then that all of the contributors demonstrate considerable courage in having their work included in an anthology that will be offensive to college and university chancellors, presidents, provosts, deans, directors, and chairs who prefer the truth be managed, manipulated, or simply mauled into silence. The unadulterated, unabridged, and uncensored truth in essays by Cayle, Christina McVay, Ben Satterfield, and David Starkey; the fiction of Jean Anderson, Richard Hill, A. L. Reilly, and Mary Rohrer-Dann; the poetry of Kat Snider Blackbird, Mark Hillringhouse, Charles Hood, Maria Theresa Maggi, Naomi Rachel, Carolyn Foster Segal, Julia Stein, and Judy Wells all confirm what the *Michigan Quarterly Review* editor wrote to me on January 13, 1993, in his rejection note for "The Only Good Writer is a Dead Writer." "I receive enough essays of this kind," Laurence Goldstein wrote, "to persuade me that something is rotten in the state of academia, not just Oregon State."

But Goldstein summarily refused all such submissions to protect the old boy and girl network. "This university's administration would not consider its flagship journal's mandate to include attacks on sister institutions." John Witte, editor of *Northwest Review,* housed and funded by the University of Oregon, echoed Goldstein's rationale for censorship when he rejected "Good Writer." Though not poorly written, the essay was "extremely bad tempered" while "on the other hand, as an instructor myself I can understand your anger and offense at the shameless exploitation of this academic underclass . . . . " Witte wrote to me on June 8, 1993, three months after Linny Stovall snapped up "Good Writer" for *Writer's N.W.,* less than a week after I sent it in. But *WNW* is not funded by or affiliated with a college or university.

And I should and will end by pointing out that the nineteen people in this anthology cannot be dismissed with that pejorative rubric "vocal minority." Meaning loud-mouthed troublemakers. But it is true that they represent a highly articulate labor group. Most exploited workers don't have the command of English this group does, nor the impressive record of publications and literary awards. And their eloquence does speak for faculty who are fast becoming the majority on campus, a statement begging support from BBIs, boring but important facts.

The U.S. Department of Education *Digest of Education Statistics* reported that the total number of non-tenured, part-time faculty (excluding graduate students) in higher education grew from 104,000 to 263,000 between 1970 and 1986. The percentage of part-timers among all faculty changed from 22% to 36% during the same period. *Academe,* the mouthpiece of the American Association of University Professors, an organization representing the privileged, tenured elite faculty on campus, reported in 1992 that universities had 25% of faculty in part-time positions, colleges 34%, and community colleges 55%. And here, finally, is a local sampling from *Crain's Cleveland Business Book of Lists* for northeastern Ohio colleges and universities in 1994. Case Western Reserve had 3% of faculty hired part-time, a big exception. Cleveland State had 32%, John Carroll University had 36%, Kent State had 46%, and the University of Akron had 54%. Local colleges ranged from one at 15% to the rest between 47% and 77%.

Nobody has stats on the number of full-time faculty in temp positions. But you can imagine.

Imagine half the teachers in your local school system hired off the street each September for full- or part-time jobs with no benefits and no future. Imagine the dedication of teachers likes Maria Maggi, A. L. Reilly, Mary Rohrer-Dann, Julia Stein, and the others in this anthology who work in a "higher" education system that would embarrass any local school board.

But before you read on, please acknowledge Kaitlin Jayne Greer, now five and the personification of humor and sanity during the two and a half years we fought to stay off the street. Fathers are blessed by daughters. Acknowledge the love and uncommon courage of my spouse, Lauren Sauvage, who had to give up an award-winning fine art career to pick teeth to support her family after Barry was fired for First Amendment use. Acknowledge the relatives who loaned us money to pay for Lauren's training as a dental hygienist (a profession that pays twice what a full-time academic peon earns). Acknowledge the Oregon Employment Division for providing unemployment checks after I was fired by OSU, checks small enough to force me to raid my pension fund to support my family while Lauren trained and I looked for work I never found. Acknowledge the wisdom of legislators who passed the law that allowed me to keep my health insurance after I was fired as long as I paid $340 a month for it. Acknowledge my former colleagues in the OSU English Department for their wisdom in assuring that a writing instructor who used the skill he taught to criticize "a supposedly democratic community of scholars" paid a price for such audacity.

Were it not for them all, this book would not exist.

Barry Greer
Corvallis, Oregon

Editor's Note: In April of 1989, an ammunition explosion destroyed a gun turret on the Iowa, a battleship built in 1943.

FORGETTING

David Ehrenfeld

The tragedy aboard the battleship Iowa is still in the newspapers as I start to write this letter, but it is probably the last day that it will be on the front page of *The New York Times.* This morning's article was about fixing the damaged gun turret--the commander of the ship says it will be difficult and might turn out to be impossible. The Iowa is of World War II vintage, and the materials and technological know-how to repair its gigantic guns may not exist anymore.

There was a similar problem about ten years ago when church officials decided it was time to resume construction of New York's vast Cathedral of St. John the Divine, after a lapse of decades. It turned out that a few old men in England were the only stone masons left in the world who knew how to work the giant blocks from which the cathedral is built. If they hadn't been able to train young apprentices, there would have been no choice but to abandon the project in a few years.

I think that our concept of progress prevents us from being aware that skills and knowledge can vanish from the world. Most of us probably imagine knowledge to be cumulative: each advance is built on prior discoveries, block piled upon block in an ever-growing edifice. We don't think of the blocks underneath as crumbling away or, worse yet, simply vanishing. Our world view doesn't prepare us for that.

Yet loss of knowledge and skills is now a big problem in our universities, and no subject is in greater danger of disappearing than our long-accumulated knowledge of the natural world. The problem is so serious that I don't hesitate to call it the next environmental crisis, although it will never rival the hole in the ozone layer or global warming for press coverage. We are on the verge of losing our ability to tell one plant or animal from another and of forgetting how the known species interact among themselves and with their environments.

The process is gradual, and it is affecting our more prestigious, research-oriented schools first. What is happening is that certain subjects no longer have anyone to teach them, or are taught on a piecemeal basis by people from the periphery of the university or outside it altogether. "Classifications of Higher Plants," "Marine Invertebrates," "Ornithology," "Mammalogy," "Cryptogams" (mosses and ferns), "Biogeography," "Comparative Physiology," "Entomology"--you may find some of them in the catalog, but too often with the notation alongside, "Not offered in 1990-91."

The features that distinguish lizards from snakes from crocodilians from turtles from tuataras aren't any less accepted or valid than they were twenty-five years ago, nor are they easier than they used to be to learn on your own from books without hands-on laboratory instructions, but try getting someone to teach such a lab in most top-ranked biology departments. There is at least one Ivy League university that is even having trouble staffing a basic ecology course from the faculty of its biology department, and as I write this there is a large, land-grant university that has no limnologist (a person who studies the biology of lakes and rivers) and only one, retired plant taxonomist on its main science campus.

New students who are attracted to the study of whole plants and animals still exist, but they find themselves in a very hostile teaching environment for their kind of biology. Not surprisingly, their numbers are dwindling. It is these students who, after getting their masters and doctoral degrees, ought to be going out to teach their subjects in the nation's colleges and universities, to be taking over as older professors retire. There won't be enough new graduates to go around. Reservoirs that are not replenished soon run dry.

To prove that I am not crying wolf, I want to tell a true story. One morning last April, at eight o'clock, my phone rang. It was a former student of mine who is now a research endocrinologist at a major teaching hospital in Houston. She had an odd question: at what point in animal evolution was the hemoglobin molecule first adopted for use specifically as an oxygen carrier? It was an essential piece of information for medical research that she was planning. If I didn't know the answer (I didn't), who did? I racked my brain to think of a contemporary biochemist or university department that could provide this answer. Nothing. All I could come up with was a book, I thought by somebody named F.A. Baldwin, that I had read when I was a student. She thanked me politely and said goodbye.

Later I went down to the basement and found the book in a box. It was *An Introduction to Comparative Biochemistry,* by Ernest (not F.A.) Baldwin, Cambridge

University Press, 1964, fourth edition--I doubt there was a fifth. The flyleaf, I noted ruefully, indicated that this hardcover text had set me back $2.75. Much of the information my former student had wanted was in there, brilliantly written.

By coincidence, I was scheduled to lecture that afternoon to a group of biochemistry professors and graduate students. So I asked them the question I had been asked earlier.."I'm not a biochemist," I said after describing the phone call. "Tell me who is working on this sort of thing these days." They looked at one another and laughed. Nobody does comparative biochemistry anymore, they answered; at least they didn't know of anybody. There probably was nothing much more recent than Baldwin. As for the graduate students, they had never even heard of comparative biochemistry.

Gone! Not outdated. Not superseded. Not scientifically or politically controversial. Not even merely frivolous. A whole continent of important human knowledge gone, like Atlantis beneath the waves. True, we still have Ernest Baldwin's book, but this kind of knowledge needs trained, experienced people to keep it alive and to hand it on to the next generation.

At nearly all of today's research colleges and universities the teaching is being done by three kinds of "temporaries": graduate students; nontenure-track researchers and scholars--mostly women--who work full-time hours for part-time pay and reduced benefits; and an assortment of experts from outside the university who free-lance courses a semester at a time. What they have in common is that they are skilled workers working for substandard wages with no job security. They tend to feel exploited and are often angry, depressed, or a mixture of the two. Some of these teachers manage to be conscientious, inspiring, and creative, but few are around for very long. Teaching, more than other professions, needs continuity.

Despite the starvation of teaching, universities are receiving and spending money as never before. Where is it going? The answer varies from school to school--at one it will be computer science, at a second genetic engineering, at a third high-energy physics--but in all cases the money is going to hire "world class scholars" at world class salaries, and to set them up in business. At my university, world class scholars have become a kind of consumer item, like fancy computer systems, and are known, collectively, as WCSls or wixels. They are purchased on the open market. One wixel can cost tens of millions of dollars by the time the university is finished providing the building, space-age equipment, and numerous support personnel that the wixel has been promised. Wixels don't have time to teach, not even graduate students.

Eventually, every asset that the administrators can lay hands on is hocked to pay for these wixels. Teaching budgets are slashed, teaching laboratories are converted into research space, and salaries of professors who are foolish enough to teach or whose research is not in one of the glamorous areas are seized when these professors retire or, if untenured, inevitably fail to gain promotion. Soon, all the university can afford to help keep its teaching program afloat is a flock of temporaries. Not only are they cheap, but if they complain they are fired.

Conventional logic would have it that killing the roots and trunk of the tree to support a few exotic flowers makes no sense. What has driven higher education into this unstable imbalance? The motive, as my readers have surely guessed, is money.

Before the Second World War, universities were run by a rather small cadre of scholars-turned-administrators, usually distinguished professors who had reached a point in their careers where pomp and affluence were more appealing than the library or laboratory. This was harmless--even useful. Every university needs a royal family to get money and charm the public. But after the war, things began to change. The Managerial Revolution was upon us, university administration became a career in itself (especially for those whose academic work wasn't going anywhere), and administrators proliferated like weeds in a garden. By the seventies and eighties, control of most universities had shifted from faculty to administration, and the ranks of administrators had grown by five- and ten-fold or more. Where did the money for expansion come from? The money came from the overhead on research grants--a postwar phenomenon--and from patents. Overhead, the amount charged by the university to administer grants, was like manna from heaven. Real administrative costs of grants are only a few percent of the total, but administrators soon discovered that they could bump up the figure to 60, 70, or even more than 100 percent of the actual research request without protest from the federal granting agencies. Better yet, the money disappeared into an administrative black hole--even the researchers who obtained the grants couldn't find out what happened to the overhead. Patent income was much the same.

There was only one catch. Grants and patents are not fixed budget items. A bloated administration required more and more of these unregulated funds to support its growth, but grants and patents are undependable.

Inevitably, universities began to bid against one another to attract those scientists (the wixels) who had the best records of getting large grants. Research priorities shifted to a few areas, such as genetic engineering, with the greatest cash flow from government and industry. Everything else, traditional research, innovative speculative research, and of course teaching, was sacrificed.

University administrators now find themselves on a treadmill that they can't get off. They must spend fortunes to gain fortunes, *but they hardly ever gain as much as they spend.* Student tuitions are raised and raised, "unproductive" departments are closed, budgets (except the wixels') are pared. Many universities, despite massive endowments and cash flows, are now little more than shells. The system is spiraling out of control.

Because similar processes are occurring throughout our society--from hospitals to secondary schools to the Department of Defense--and because we have squandered most of the natural resources that gave us our wealth, we will soon run out of money to support the Managerial Revolution, and it will end. But abrupt, unplanned endings mean chaos, which nobody wants. How can we brake the administrative juggernaut before it crashes? This is one of the major unsolved problems confronting society. The only solution I can think of starts by drastically reducing the flow of money to administration--soon. There is no reason why unspecified grant overheads should exceed 8 or 10 percent. In the case of heavily endowed schools, there should also be an end to knee-jerk giving by wealthy alumni, especially contributions for new buildings. In the modern university, money is increasingly proving to be a corrosive substance.

Turning off the money tap is not enough, however. An informed public will have to demand cuts in administration, greater faculty and student influence, a tuition freeze, a moratorium on construction of "high tech" facilities, a higher priority for teaching, and support for a diversity of low-cost research projects which can function without multimillion-dollar grants and which may not generate lucrative patents.

And if there is no effective change, what then? Then we can expect the managerial ethic to continue to prevail and teaching to become vestigial as the existing university structure falls further into disarray. True, a new kind of university may emerge, perhaps already is emerging. It will have some positive features. But whatever its virtues, it will not be capable of transmitting our assembled knowledge of the natural world to the next generation. I fear for conservation when there is no one left in our places of learning who can tell one moth from another, no one who knows the habits of hornbills, no one to puzzle over the diversity of hawthorns.

Reprinted from Orion, *Autumn 1989, with permission of Orion and the author. A revised version of this and other essays on related themes was published in* Beginning Again: People and Nature in the New Millennium, *by David Ehrenfeld (Oxford University Press, 1993).*

LOWER THAN THE LOW ONE ON THE TOTEM POLE: TEACHING WRITING TO OREGON COLLEGE STUDENTS

M. Elizabeth Wallace

Over the past year, I have talked to all of the non-tenure-track English instructors and lecturers who teach the single most important course in our state colleges and universities: Freshman Composition. And I have come to what seem to be two contradictory conclusions: these instructors are doing a wonderful job (Oregon's students are well-served); and the situation is disgraceful (in the long run, our students are not well-served at all).

An instructor at the University of Oregon gave me the image for this paradox. He said, "We instructors are not the low men and women on the totem pole. We are the part deep underground, holding the whole thing up." What he did not go on to say, but what seems to me obvious from my year's research, is that this strong but unseen foundation is being attacked by worms and parasites and fungi, being slowly eaten away, and lest we take care, the entire structure will topple, undermined by the rotting system below.

But why should anyone take me seriously? I've already said at least one ridiculous thing, that Freshman Composition is the single most important course taught at our state colleges and universities. Everyone knows that senior seminars in one's major field play a much more crucial role in one's intellectual and professional life. Freshman writing teaches no real content; it merely perfects a skill one should have acquired earlier. In fact, it's embarrassing that our state colleges and universities have to teach it at all. Right? Wrong.

Only those who reduce Freshman Composition to the insertion of commas and the healing of split infinitives could justify such an attitude. Granted, a nationwide influx of seemingly illiterate freshman in the early seventies, students ill-prepared for college-level writing tasks, required the sudden restructuring of English curriculums across the country to deal with the problem. But the faculty who threw themselves into freshman writing courses and began to explore the writing process itself moved into uncharted territory. Suddenly they were studying not just classical rhetoric and grammar, but cognitive psychology, epistemology, philosophy of science and the sociology of knowledge. They became fascinated by creative processes, by how we both build and discover our knowledge and often don't seem to know a thing until we say it, yet don't struggle to say it unless we feel we know it. They became perplexed along the borderline between knowledge we truly have but cannot ever put into words or formulae (recognizing a friend's face, riding a bicycle) and knowledge we don't seem to have until we find the language for it (like Eliza Doolittle in *Pygmalion).*

The past fifteen years have transformed the discipline of writing. Professional societies devoted to the teaching of writing have flourished, among them the Conference on College Composition and Communication (affectionately known as 4 C's), The Council of Writing Program Administrators (WPA) and The Association of Teachers of Technical Writing (ATTW). Further, the traditional associations for English teachers like MLA

(Modern Language Association), NCTE (National Council of Teachers of English), ADE (Association of Departments of English) and CEA (College English Association), which once focused almost entirely on literary history and criticism, have enormously extended the attention paid to writing theory and practice. MLA, in particular, has formulated guidelines for the professional treatment of teachers of writing, arguing that publication and research in the teaching of writing should count equally with literary scholarship in hiring, tenure and promotion decisions. New PhD's in rhetoric, unlike most new PhD's in literature, find themselves eagerly sought after by employers.

I do not mean to imply that we now are able to teach *right* something we heretofore had always taught *wrong*. As a rule Freshman Composition has never been taught simply to correct mechanical errors, although there was and still is too much of that. Rather, a mysterious process--a process that accomplished teachers always knew to be crucial to the intellectual development of their students--is now receiving more direct attention than ever before. No one is quite sure how much of the tacit act by which we invest words with meaning can or ever should be made fully explicit. We only know that the way we use language--understood broadly as the various symbol systems of our culture-- and the ways we are created by it from birth determine all the discoveries we will ever be able to make or share with others.

In Freshman Composition students explore their immersion in language and acknowledge that from the moment they spoke a first word, they began to take on the minds of others. Every language is a framework of assumptions about the nature of reality, and Freshman

Comp both uses and challenges that framework. Instructors ponder with students the ethics of persuasion, manipulation, euphemism, advertisement, fact, fiction, conflict and sentimentality. Comp is a meditation on how thoughts both do and don't exist before they are expressed and on how selves both do and don't exist before *they* are expressed. The teacher of writing leads a long experiment in discovering what one knows and doesn't know--by taking risks with words, by trusting the generative power of syntax, hearing the voices in our heads, rushing to write them down and then ruthlessly editing them later on. The college writing course is an apprenticeship in how we shape and extend the powers of language while language simultaneously shapes us.

Thus the chief qualifications for a teacher of writing, besides the ability to enter sympathetically into the thoughts of others, is a belief in the reality and power of written language. And the best evidence for such a belief is writing itself, everything from letters and novels to press releases and sale brochures. Studying writing with a teacher who doesn't write is like studying swimming with a teacher who doesn't swim--when you finally try to test the theory in practice, you may drown.

Luckily, according to an articulate theorist in the composition field (Louise Wetherbee Phelps, director of the new writing program at Syracuse University), the staffing of our writing programs in Oregon may already be the best it could possibly be. Phelps argues that the single *worst* way to build a writing program would be to hire a complete cadre of PhD's in rhetoric, career academics. Such homogeneity in staffing would destroy the one thing students most need to see--the wide range of *real* purposes writing serves. Students need to know that their writing faculty includes not only published literary scholars but novelists, poets, film and theatre reviewers, political activists, sports columnists, hopeful playwrights, unpublished humorists, private journal writers, authors of computer manuals or advertising copy, and graduate students struggling with dissertations.

We have such a range of writers in Oregon. In fact, because of its astonishing landscape, Oregon attracts more than its fair share of bright, articulate folk who are in love with beauty and eagerly write about it--from essays on fly fishing to philosophical meditations on the puny human figure dwarfed against a panorama of forest, field, volcano and sky.

So where's the problem? What do I find so disgraceful? That we seem to be systematically doing everything we can to destroy these energetic writers and teachers. Frequently the only kind of encouragement they feel is to leave Oregon or, at the very least, to leave the teaching profession.

How to destroy a writing program

The formula is simple. Ignoring degrees, publications or teaching experience, pay writing instructors a low flat rate per course. Give course assignments a week or two before term and refuse any suggestion of job security from year to year; in fact, occasional reminders of how precarious their teaching assignments are (and how many other qualified people would love to have them) will significantly lower complaints about working conditions.

Ignoring all the research that has been done in the last ten years on the successful management of part-time and short-term faculty, continue to treat those instructors like second-class citizens; make no effort to get to know them; don't introduce them officially at department and faculty meetings when they are tlrst hired; · offer no orientation to the campus, the curriculum, the department, or support services and staff; deny them access to faculty development funds or at least keep their eligibility for such funds a secret for as long as possible; refuse them leave without pay, sabbaticals and promotions; pay them less per course than the graduate teaching fellows that they are sometimes asked to take on as apprentices; strictly limit the kinds of courses they are allowed to teach; and never consider seriously their applications for any full-time tenure-track job openings in the department. Further, define a full-time load for an instructor or lecturer so heavy that they'll have no time or energy for any reading and writing of their own, let alone collegiality with their fellows (which might, after all, lead to union organizing or other forms of group political action).

No one institution in Oregon commits all of these crimes at once, and some are much better than others at treating instructors as true colleagues; but all of these crimes are committed in our state year after year. English departments are not the only departments where such abuses occur, but in Oregon, as in the rest of the United States, they account for most of the non-standard undergraduate faculty appointments, primarily in the teaching of writing. Other big users of part-time and short-term faculty are foreign languages, mathematics and business/economics. However, business/economics part-time faculty tend to teach only one or two classes a year because they have full-time jobs outside academia. Humanities non-tenure-track faculty, on the other hand, seldom have careers elsewhere; most of their income, benefits and professional identity come from their teaching positions.

And what a professional identity it is! The

average full-time writing instructor in this state puts in at least a 70-hour work week. How do I figure that? Consider the needs of the student: as a *minimal* standard, one might hope that a student taking an 11-week course in writing might be asked to write a few pages each week--perhaps one short weekly essay or rough draft. Also, it seems reasonable to expect that student to receive approximately 30 minutes of attention from the instructor each week--enough time for the instructor to read those pages attentively and either write down some comments and suggestions or meet in conference with the student to discuss the student's further plans for the piece.

A full-time instructor's load is usually four courses a quarter or 12 courses a year (at U. of O., ten courses a year); if each course is in freshman writing, that means (by Oregon guidelines) 25 students per class, or 100 per quarter. In addition to the 12 hours an instructor teaches each week (each course meets three hours a week), and a bare minimum of eight hours of class preparation and obligatory office hours (we'll omit, for the moment, hours spent in department or committee meetings), the teacher must spend 50 hours per week reading and commenting on student writing--a 70-hour work week! Needless to say, not much time is left over for staying current in one's field, let alone researching and writing an article or writing anything else.

What about pay? Consider the pay scale and workload for non-tenure-track faculty in the English department at Southern Oregon State College. One can have a doctorate and three books to one's credit and still earn only $900 per writing course at SOSC. A full-time lecturer's load is five courses per quarter, upping our estimated work-week to 85 hours. A lecturer managing

15 courses a year would earn $13,500 (or just under $5 an hour). (Compare this with the *starting* salary of an MA teaching the same courseload at Chemeketa Community College in Salem: $22,203). And since SOSC's $900 salary per three-credit-hour course hasn't increased a penny in the past five years, we are *negatively* rewarding years of teaching experience and loyalty to the institution. Apparently cost-of-living increases or faculty raises approved by the legislature don't find their way into the paychecks needing them most.

Before we tax-weary voters protest that faculty can make lots of money at summer jobs and over Christmas and spring break, remember that faculty are still grading final exams and papers long after students have left at end of term and are usually preparing courses and syllabi weeks before the beginning of the term--besides, most jobs available over the summer are similar to the insecure teaching jobs they already hold: part-time at minimum wage. Moveover, Oregon law does not allow teachers to collect unemployment over the summer, and summer school positions pay no better than regular term teaching.

Of course, most college teachers enter the profession *expecting* 70-hour work weeks during the term and *not* expecting to get rich. But they *don't* expect, after ten years of teaching experience and conscientious work, to be eligible for food stamps and welfare.

Is it any wonder that so many instructors working under conditions described above leave Oregon to teach elsewhere or leave the teaching profession entirely? Only the most hare-brained idealists would continue to put in 70-80 hour work weeks for such low wages in positions that lead nowhere. Instead, instructors who stay make compromises with their own convictions about how writing courses should be taught: perhaps they assign less writing, read assignments less closely, or cut back on conferences with students.

Indeed, how can we pretend to boast about the quality of higher education in Oregon when we don't even pay lip service to the basic recommendations of two national professional associations--NCTE and ADE--that freshman writing be held to no more than 20 students per class?

What we do right

Is there anything good about the way Oregon treats writing instructors? Yes. Portland State University, the University of Oregon and Western Oregon State College have received praise from instructors for real efforts at collegiality. A lecturer who has taught at almost every community college and state university in the Willamette Valley over the past six years (he usually has to teach part-time at two or three places simultaneously in order to support himself) recently praised WOSC for doing three things *no other college had done during all his years of teaching in Oregon:* writing to welcome him to the college, inviting him to the luncheon for new faculty (during which he received some helpful orientation to the institution) and officially introducing him at a faculty meeting. Such things may not put food on the table but neither do they cost the state of Oregon much money--and they certainly help the new part-time faculty member feel like a valued member of a professional community.

Instructors also never forget a department chair or writing program director who respects their hard work and speaks up for their right to fairer treatment. At the University of Oregon, a new director of composition organized workshops on the teaching of writing for new instructors in the fall; further, the department chair backed the instructors' request for reduced courseloads and more equitable compensation.   Part-timers at Portland State tell, as a kind of legend, the story of their previous writing program director's stand for them. Part-time and untenured herself, she was asked to take on the task of directing the writing program full-time several years ago but refused--unless she be allowed to offer the majority of her part-time faculty contracts for halftime or more at the beginning of each academic year (such a contract permits the granting of most benefits in the state system, particularly medical benefits.)   Not many *tenured* faculty take such risks for their part-time' colleagues--but she put her career on the line and won her point.

That story illustrates another thing Oregon does better than some states in its treatment of English instructors: making benefits, particularly medical benefits, available to those teaching halftime and above.   The universities are doing better at this than the state colleges, although an effort has been made recently at SOSC, for instance, to assign courses earlier so that part-time faculty know if they qualify for medical coverage.   But administrative policies vary from place to place; occasionally, a conscious effort is made to keep every part-timer's schedule *below* halftime as a cost-saving measure, avoiding the expense of benefits.   The situation is further complicated by the fact that the very definition of halftime can vary from time to time and from place to place.

Benign neglect also plays a role: instructors are sometimes eligible for benefits and don't know it. In the absence of clear procedures for orientation and supervision, everyone assumes that someone else has informed the new faculty members about various support services and benefits available to them--everything from photocopying to parking privileges--when in fact no one has.

The past year has seen some improvement for instructors in another area--support for faculty development and continuing education. In this decade, for an instructor to be out of touch with recent developments in the teaching of writing is to impoverish self and students. Only one year ago, the few instructors who attended workshops or conferences on the teaching of writing said they did so at their own expense. But since then, several instructors have made modest, successful requests for workshop registration fees and in-state travel funds; and the recently appointed composition director at Oregon State encouraged four writing instructors to attend either a national 4 C's convention or a workshop on Writing Across the Curriculum and found institutional funding for them to do so. Professional development funds are some of the best investments any institution or business can make because they tend to release energy and creativity that in turn nurture the institution itself.

Finally, Oregon does not place a cap on the number of years an instructor can teach at a particular college or university. Oregon State used to, resulting in the odd necessity for teachers to disappear periodically at regular intervals (every three years) and somehow manage to support themselves until they could be re-employed the following year.

Anomalies

Odd contradictions exist around the state. While the University of Oregon has in place the best promotion scheme for instructors, allowing them to progress in salary and status year by year until they qualify for consideration as a senior instructor in their sixth year, all six other institutions pay instructors a flat rate across the board, almost uniformly ignoring years of service. At SOSC, degrees have no influence on salary per course; at OIT, they do. Publications and professional papers presented don't seem to affect salaries for instructors anywhere (probably on the assumption that an instructorship is defined entirely as a teaching position--though as we've established, teachers of writing who don't themselves write are something of a contradiction in terms).

Another anomaly--everywhere except at EOSC, Writing 121 is considered a three-credit course. At EOSC, along the lines wisely suggested by Donald McQuade at MLA in 1982, Writing 121 is a five-credit course. This accomplishes several intelligent things at once: it often reduces the courseload for full-time faculty members teaching 121, allowing them to give extra time to student writing and individual conferences; it reinforces, in student and faculty minds alike, the importance of the course and recognizes the unusual investment of time and energy it requires; and it allows part-time faculty teaching the course to be compensated more fairly, since they are paid by the credit hour. One of the best things every English department in the state could do to upgrade the teaching of writing and better reward those who teach it would be to define Writing 121 as a five-credit course immediately.

Rank and pay around the state are confusing in their variety and irrational contradictions. Local market factors seem to play a large part, although it is difficult to understand why a part-time instructor with an MA should earn $900 per course at OIT and twice that at

Oregon State (where a much larger pool of qualified instructors exists.) Of course, the common factor is that neither one is paid fairly.

What we can fix

If I were to list the major problems with our treatment of English instructors statewide, I would start with the geographical factor. Only 18.7 percent of the writing instructors teaching spring quarter 1987 maintained that geography played *no* part in their decision to teach in Oregon; 21.3 percent stated that they chose to live in Oregon first and then search for work. But 60 percent said that they were absolutely restricted to a particular area in their search for employment, at least for the present.

Much is made in academia of the difference between hiring procedures for tenure-track college faculty (chosen from a national search) and instructors (chosen from a local search). Those who choose to settle in Oregon at any cost are often at a disadvantage in their search for academic jobs, simply because they are already here: academia much prefers to interview exotic strangers from across the country. But at least job seekers who *choose* to live here know what they're doing and to that extent accept responsibility for their predicament.

However, those who arrive in Eugene, Portland, La Grande, Klamath Falls, Ashland, Monmouth or Corvallis following a spouse to a full-time job or coming to care for a sick relative or following children in the custody of a divorced partner have automatically removed themselves from the national academic job market and have entered the local market with no choice in the matter. Overcoming that single obstacle is sometimes impossibly difficolt, no matter what one's qualifications might be. Once one accepts that first course assignment, perhaps advertised in *The Register Guard,* one is assumed to be a "bad hire"--in administrative lingo, someone who doesn't meet all affirmative action guidelines (because the position was not advertised nationally) and whose credentials must be suspect because they come from a local pool.

Occasionally superior scholars and teachers have been hired out of the instructor pool onto the tenure track (it has happened twice at the University of Oregon in the past ten years), but instructors who hang on hoping for this to happen are probably being unrealistic. Much could be done to correct the current inequities if all instructor positions, full- and part-time, were nationally advertised and all required procedures for a standard search were followed--despite the fact that national searches are expensive and time-consuming procedures. At the very least, changing hiring practices in this way would guarantee that an entire committee (and the committee should, of course, include other writing instructors), rather than just a harried department chair or writing program director, would read and be familiar with the credentials of newly appointed English instructors. Instructors who have taught for eight years at the University of Oregon on occasion have been mistaken for graduate students or janitors by their colleagues; such invisibility hardly strengthens faculty morale.

Closely linked with the geographical issue is the sexism of the situation, but it is a complicated form of sexism. One Oregon professor was heard to refer repeatedly to instructors in his department, one-third of whom were men, as "placebound little old ladies in hats and tennis shoes." The assumption dies hard that writing can be taught by anyone who speaks English and

who has the leisure and volunteer spirit to teach it--
hence, faculty wives. Apart from the fact that faculty
wives these days--as physicians and lawyers or
accountants--are apt to be earning considerably more
than their husbands and to be at least as highly educated,
this inappropriate caricature ignores the growing reality
of faculty husbands as well as single, divorced or
widowed parents who support themselves and their
families entirely by their instructor teaching jobs.

In the spring quarter of 1987, 59 percent of all
English instructors at Oregon state colleges and
universities were women; a year later, the figure was
closer to 66 percent, primarily because of a shift at the
University of Oregon. This percentage is much more
revealing when one considers that only 20 percent of all
tenured or tenure-track English faculty in the state are
women.

The situation is compounded by infrequent hirings at
the professorial level. For instance, until the spring of
1988, WOSC had gone 16 years without hiring anyone
onto the tenure track in English. The University of
Oregon has lost 15 full-time tenure-track positions since
the late sixties, at a time when the student body steadily
grew. Oregon is not unique in this respect: colleges
across the country stopped hiring in the late sixties and
early seventies, awaiting the projected severe drop in
enrollments. It never came. Meanwhile, college and
university administrators developed some very bad habits
and learned how cheaply they could acquire part-time the
devoted services of new and unemployed PhD's who
were desperate for anything resembling a teaching
career.

In fact, most of the few recent tenure-track
appointments in English statewide have gone to women,
contributing to the growing phenomenon of husbands

with PhD's following their wives' careers. Thus the sexism of the English instructor situation should be defined carefully, in the following way: behaviors traditionally associated with women in our society-- putting one's own career on hold while a spouse develops his or hers, allowing geographical limitations to determine one's search for employment, or teaching part-time while raising children or caring for invalid relatives--play an important role in restricting one to peripheral faculty status.

Instructors in Oregon must also contend with the seemingly universal obsession with the PhD as the sole document that qualifies one for the tenure-track teaching of writing. Not that many of them don't have one--25 percent do and another 20 percent have coursework or degrees *beyond* the MA (only two writing instructors in the state system have anything less than an MA). Much more significant for the teaching they are doing, however, is the fact that 68 percent of them are publishing writers. If Richard Marins, the director of the expository writing program at Harvard, can argue that his part-time faculty deserve a starting salary of $5200 (plus benefits) for each class of 15 students-- primarily on the grounds that they write continually and are paid to publish their work (everything from book reviews to sports columns to science fiction)--then perhaps Oregon colleges and universities could dare to declare the same--that writing and publication, *not* the PhD, are the qualifying credentials for teaching writing.

Another problem is also universal to all seven of the state colleges and universities: English instructors and lecturers are encouraged in every way possible *not* to see their teaching here as a career. Besides the obvious encouragement to leave represented by low pay, heavy course loads, large classes, last-minute hirings, lack of support for faculty development, impossibility of promotion, and exclusion from faculty governance and social functions, instructors are (even if with the best intentions) frequently told that they should not confuse their instructorships with a real profession.

It should be abundantly clear by now that a self-fulfilling prophecy is at work: the writing instructor is encouraged on all fronts to reflect, "Get out--this is a burn-out position. You can't build a career on this." But the teaching of *the single most important course in our state colleges and universities need not* be a burn-out profession. All that we have to do is decide to value and support it and create the working conditions that make excellence and growth and the retention of dedicated, experienced faculty a possibility.

In a state system, the voters share the blame

One philosophy of educational staffing maintains that all available money should be directed toward the hiring of top guns, stars in literary criticism and research who will attract undergraduates and graduates students alike to matriculate at our colleges and universities. But the opposing view has perhaps been put best by Wayne Booth, past president of MLA and the George M. Pullman Professor of English at the University of Chicago:

> You can tell whether a college is serious about teaching its students at any level simply by looking closely at how many freshman are taught by part-time faculty members . . . who have no stake in the future of the institution and its programs, no sense of how their work relates to anything else the college is doing, no long-

range prospect of full-time or permanent employment, and thus little reason to think that what they do matters to anyone. . . . The composition course could in fact become a center of intellectual vitality for a whole campus.
. . . In short, any college that takes seriously the problem of how to teach writing will become intellectually alive, and any college that is intellectually alive will automatically train and integrate its part-time faculty.

By Booth's standard, we're not doing very well. Yet according to Louise Wetherbee Phelps, we may be close to having the best kind of writing program there is, one consisting primarily of faculty who care about teaching, who write often themselves for a wide variety of audiences and purposes, and who can therefore enrich and challenge each other as well as their students.

So I'm back to my original contradiction, and what now seems clear is the turning point we've reached. Depending on our next move, we can make higher education in Oregon much better or much worse. So far, because of the quality of *most* of our freshmen writing instructors, we're managing much better than we have any right to expect. But we also are losing talented writer/scholar/teachers every year who, but for truly professional treatment and a decent increment in pay, could have been persuaded to continue in what Booth calls "the single most important task any of us faces" --transforming "those confused and semi-literate freshmen souls into alert, curious, and effective writers." We have two alternatives. We can begin to take advantage of the situation and nurture and support the fine teachers we have. Or we can continue to do what we've done so far--take advantage not of the situation but of the faculty themselves, exploiting as much as we can the very qualities that make them valuable to us and that make them vulnerable: their love of teaching, reading, writing--and Oregon. We can eat away at those qualities until English instructors find themselves drained and hollow, needing to escape at any cost to save their sanity and self-respect.

And then the totem pole can come crashing down as we rush to replace them, to shore up the very foundations of our educational system--a belief in the reality and importance of language and the written word.

First published in Sweet Reason, *1988.*

PAPER GRADERS

Barry Greer

At the University of Oregon they're called paper graders, little old ladies in sneakers, and trailing spouses. At other universities, they're called anything from migrant workers to academic gypsies, suitcase teachers, MIAs, Kelly girls, and comp (composition) dogs. They teach in fine arts, music, English, Russian, Romance languages, East Asian languages, history, math, psychology, business, education, computer science, biology, in nearly every University of Oregon department.

They're part of the part-timer problem, a term used in higher education with the same tone as "the Palestinian problem," "the apartheid problem," or "the poverty problem." The problem is the result of a callous and calculated policy in the 1980s to save a buck by using up well-educated, highly motivated, dedicated college teachers like so many throw-away parts. A mind used to be a terrible thing to waste. Not in the '80s, not at the University of Oregon. Wear one out, buy another. UCLA researcher Emily Abel, quoted by *Time,* said, "They're like any part-time employees that McDonald's would hire . . . cheap labor that colleges and universities are relying on to save money."

That was the excuse during the recession early in the decade, but once education administrators found they could keep 30 percent of their work force in poorly paid, insecure positions, abusing people to save a buck or two became habit. A permanent underclass, what the

American Federation of Teachers (AFT) calls "academic slave labor," was created when the bosses learned they could hire or fire on whim at will.

Norman Wessells, University of Oregon provost and the man with the most power on campus to affect academic hiring policy, estimated most UO instructors were part-timers, and said that they're not eligible for tenure, that their pay is lousy, that the job has a high turnover rate. Wessells estimated the number at UO to be 175. According to the UO Office of Institutional Research, during fall term, 1989, instructors made up 159 of 919 teaching faculty. (The number has been as high as 300 this decade.) If non-tenure-track assistant professors are included, 30 percent of UO teaching faculty is hired year to year or term to term. Thirty-five percent of all teaching faculty aren't regular. Sixty percent of instructors are women, the highest percentage of any academic rank, a percentage that shrinks the higher the rank. Assistant profs: 45 percent. Associate profs: 28 percent. Full professor: 11 percent women. So much for affirmative action.

But instructors are only teachers. Wessells stressed more than once during my interview with him that the University of Oregon was a research institution. He's right, and his point is an important one to understand to get at an even more fundamental motive for using slave labor.

*

Research and the status generated by research--that's he product sold at corporate universities like the University of Oregon. Research generates grant money. Research builds a scholar's reputation, a department's reputation, a university's reputation, a university president's reputation. Teaching doesn't mean shit. One UO tenured professor, himself an award-winning teacher, drilled that point into our thick graduate student skulls in a requisite research methods seminar. Socrates couldn't get tenure at the University of Oregon.

"The motive," Rutgers University professor David Ehrenfeld wrote in *Orion*, "is money." The Managerial Revolution reached higher ed and "university administration became a career in itself (especially for those whose academic work wasn't going anywhere), and administrators proliferated like weeds in a garden." Grant money fertilized the weeds. "There was only one catch. Grants and patents were not fixed budget items. A bloated administration required more and more of these unregulated funds to support its growth, but grants and patents are undependable." Now what?

The higher a university's status in the national market, the more state, federal, and corporate funding (investment) generated. The more money the University of Oregon gets, the more money it has to pay high-priced salaries for researchers with big reps to do their work at UO, which creates more status to get more money to buy more status. "Inevitably, universities began to bid against one another to attract those scientists . . . who had the best records of getting large grants," said Ehrenfeld. Bidding pushed salaries and perks through the roof. The same old story of greed and glory.

Academics call it the star system, a system of vicious competition to get a big rep and a big salary. Ehrenfeld calls these academic yuppies "wixels," for WCSis, World Class Scholars. "At my university, world class scholars have become a consumer item, like fancy computer systems . . . . They're purchased on the open market. One wixel can cost tens of millions of dollars by the time the university is finished providing the building, space-age equipment, and numerous support personnel that the wixel has been promised."

But that's Rutgers, a big league school. "The fundamental problem at the University of Oregon," said Provost Wessells, "is funding." But the university found money for the new science complex, paid for with $45 million in state and federal tax dollars-- $33.4 million from U.S. Department of Energy and $12 million from the Oregon lottery. And then there's the Riverfront Research Park. UO president Myles Brand told *Old Oregon,* the UO alumni magazine, that "as a comprehensive research institution . . . the University of Oregon places strong emphasis on research programs in the most advanced areas of basic science."

A 1986 Carnegie Foundation for the Advancement of Teaching study argued that "investment in teaching is the key ingredient in the building of a successful institution." *Old Oregon* reported that building the science complex created *550* construction jobs in Eugene for three years. That equals the annual salary of 833 full-time instructors for three years.

The Carnegie study also found that 70 percent of university professors preferred not to teach. David Ehrenfeld agrees. "Wixels don't have time to teach, not even graduate students."

*

But who does the teaching? That's like asking why auto workers work in Detroit. The university creates its own supply of cheap labor. "At nearly all research colleges and universities," said Ehrenfeld, "the teaching is being done by three kinds of temporaries: graduate students; nontenure track researchers and scholars [instructors]--mostly women--who work full-time hours for part-time pay and reduced benefits; and an assortment of experts [called adjunct instructors or adjunct professors at UO] who free-lance courses a semester at a time. What they have in common is that they are skilled workers working for substandard wages with no job security." Which means they "tend to feel exploited and are often angry, depressed, or a mixture of the two. Some of these teachers manage to be conscientious, inspiring, and creative, but few are around for very long."

UO enrollment was 17,800 for fall term, 1989--13,800 undergraduates and 4,000 graduate students. Many UO scholars do teach (and some are excellent), but most of the lower division undergraduate courses are taught by one of the 1,140 graduate teaching assistants (GTFs) or by an instructor hired at the last minute. Part-timers get piece work, pay by the course. Those given work full-time earn, though most have a master's or doctoral degree, the same as the starting pay for a teacher with a bachelor's degree in Eugene's 4-J school district, around $18,000 a year. Some UO departments pay as little as $15,000-17,000.

UO wixels get paid $40,000-45,000 in the humanities or social sciences, and in the glamour sciences--physics and chemistry--they gross up to $70,000 a year. (The median family income in Oregon in $29,000.) Still they whine about not getting enough money and throw the usual tantrum if they don't get more: give me a raise or I'll take my lab and leave. A Ph.D. with 15 years' experience in 4-J earns $38,000, but then, a wixel would say, they don't do research, do they? A UO instructor with a Ph.D. and 15 years' experience would still earn starting pay. But, then, they don't do research, do they?

And the rich get richer. The late Richard Hill, UO provost at the time he testified at a 1987 Employment Relations Board (ERB) hearing, said regular professors recommend their own raises within broad guidelines written by the Chancellor's office. The wixels in one department mentioned at the hearing voted themselves a 10 percent jump in salary. Instructors got whatever was left, a trickle-down of about three percent, less than a cost of living increase.

That meant a $40,000-a-year wixel got a $4,000 raise while the $18,000-a-year instructor got a $540 raise. The rationale given by Hill for such a ludicrous discrepancy was that "the decision was made to make an effort to retain in Oregon a class of faculty that were employed in what were defined as high demand, highly competitive areas."

"What the president and I," said Norman Wessells when asked him what the UO plans to do about instructor pay, "want to do . . . is to see what the bill is, to get as close as we can to equitable--equitable is the word--to an appropriate living wage, whatever you want to call it, and make plans on how to get there." Right now, "equitable" means those who teach are worth no more than what they need to live on, if that.

*

If knowing they're considered almost worthless isn't bad enough, instructors also have to put up with constant insult. Wessells said instructors usually don't have the qualifications needed to be an assistant professor, the entry level tenure-track position that leads to all the perks. But, said Wessells, who's been in higher education for a quarter century, he had "a feeling" instructors were "highly regarded" in departments where they teach. "Anybody who understands what goes on in freshman writing and calculus and Romance languages has respect for what these people are doing for the institution. We couldn't survive without instructors."

But Wessells conceded that instructors get trapped into teaching positions and can't move up into better paying research faculty ranks because of what he called "the structure" of the position. This is how "the structure" works. Each department counts the number of students who sign up for lower division courses (called "sections") at the beginning of each term. The department has a certain number of grad students (some just given a book and told to go teach) to cover the sections but not enough to cover them all and no tenured prof will stoop to teach extra sections. At that point a department administrator goes to the slave market for instructors. During the ERB hearing, one instructor said that "even as late as the day before classes begin I've gotten assigned to courses during Mac Court registration."

A few instructors are hired from year to year full-time if enrollment remains more or less the same. The full-timers are given a nonbinding promise (that's right, a promise that isn't a promise) that they'll be rehired the next year. But the promise has nothing to do with creating job continuity. It's used to prevent an instructor from collecting unemployment benefits when she's laid off.

In the 1980s, the UO began using a Machiavellian personnel practice originally meant to prevent public school teachers from collecting unemployment benefits during summer vacations, the rationale being that school teachers always went back to work in the fall. But a UO instructor never knows each June if the job will still be available the next September. A UO department can simply not rehire an instructor if enrollment drops or if enough graduate students are around to teach (a rare occurrence).

John Duncan, president of the AFT union organizing committee and now an Oregon expatriate, said at the ERB hearings that early in the 1980s instructors "received no information [on rehiring] at all. The next summer . . . I realized that something was wrong with the system and began collecting unemployment during the first three months in which I was actually unemployed. I did this again another summer and then someone someplace figured out that they could, I suppose, save money" and Duncan could no longer collect unemployment during the summer even though he had no job waiting for him the next September.

The policy also allows the UO to arbitrarily fire an instructor at any time, and the practice, says David Ehrenfeld, allows a university to fire any instructor who complains.

One instructor I interviewed, an expert on minority education, in spite of an excellent record, got fired after six years. Her department chair told her they didn't need any more instructors. Nothing else, just that: we don't need you any more.

Another, an instructor lucky enough to work full-time, said: "I am a good teacher who provides an essential service to the . . . university for a measly $18,000 a year. I have taught . . . at UO for 10 years and consistently received good-to-excellent evaluations from over 2,500 students, as well as my faculty evaluators, but cannot afford to send either of my college-age daughters to the university. I have tried to effect positive change for my rank, spending virtually years working with other instructors and negotiating with university administrators but getting nowhere. Regardless of how much my students appreciate me or the fulfillment I experience teaching, I am a fool to stay."

Another single parent with two kids I talked to is hired each fall for nine months with a contract that requires her to commit to the job from September to June but allows her department to fire her for no reason at the end of any term. She gets one course a term and one course in the summer for $6,600 a year and no health insurance.

The federal poverty level for a single parent with two kids is $9,100. Having to hustle all the time to find money to make ends meet, she has no time for the research she needs to do to find a better job elsewhere, and she's been told that she'll never get a better job at the University of Oregon if she doesn't go elsewhere first. If she did find time to do research, she wouldn't be given a space in the UO library because she's not hired to do research.

The job is "structured" to drive instructors out of the job. Provost Wessells said three to five years is the usual time in the position before people "move on," as they say in academia. To what? For what? The high turnover rate allows the university to bring in "new blood," says Wessells, a ghoulish term for younger teachers with new ideas. From the instructors' point of view, it means people who haven't figured out that they're being used yet.

The high turnover also allows the university to

continue an old form of higher ed nepotism masked now as a progressive solution for the "trailing spouse" or "dual career" problem. The UO usually offers an instructor position to a wixel or administrator's "trailing spouse" unless the wixel has a national reputation or happens to be in top administration. Peg Brand, described in *Old Oregon* as "a teacher of philosophy," is the trailing spouse of UO president Myles Brand. Peg is now a professor in the UO Philosophy Department.

The trailing spouse has secure employment as long as she or he stays married. The only other guarantee of longevity in the instructor position is to become a toady or indispensable to a department somehow. "We have had instructors and senior instructors with the university for 30 years," testified Richard Hill on June 11, 1987. Indispensable and silent.

*

But in 1984, the University of Oregon instructors spoke out. For the next three years they worked with considerable courage and diligence for a vote to affiliate with the American Federation of Teachers. On March 27, 1987, the AFT petitioned the ERB to form a union. The Oregon State System of Higher Education (OSSHE) and the University of Oregon fought the petition every step of the way, but the instructors had the upper hand after the June 11 hearing.

Hearing testimony established that instructors were a class of workers separate from and unequal to regular faculty. Hearings officer William Greer issued a strong recommendation on August 7, 1987 for an ERB-ordered union election. He wrote that "the subject employees have numerous, significant differences in wages, hours

- 45 -

and other working conditions." One AFT organizer excitedly told a colleague, "We won!" The confidence level was so high that the AFT even began to work to form an Oregon State University union.

But on November 17, 1987, instructors received a letter from the AFT that began with: "Your right to self-determination in terms of collective bargaining has been denied."

Four sources, including two AFT officials, told me that an ERB reversal of the hearing officer's decision was "highly unusual" and a "political deal" because the hearings officer checks with the board before writing an order, a complex document requiring serious legal research. One source alleged unethical and possibly illegal discussions between ERB members and OSSHE officials.

Union activists didn't give up, but their efforts became desparate. Union organizer John Duncan and AFT official Ron Melton arranged a meeting with then-UO president Paul Olum. In a long conversation with me in late November, 1987, Ron Melton described what happened in the meeting. He told me at the time to remain silent about the information for fear of jeopardizing John Duncan's job and my job. But Duncan is gone. Melton described Olum as "hostile" and said the meeting finally came down to the real issue, the malignant core of the instructor problem. Power. Olum didn't want to share it. He wouldn't allow the union on his campus.

Since then, life has gotten even tougher for University of Oregon instructors. Eleven of the 30 instructors on the list of AFT union activists I was shown can't be found in the University of Oregon 1989-1990 phone directory. MIAs.

Instructors in the UO English Department, where the drive to form a union began, are running scared. One instructor told me that any information distributed among instructors always found its way into the hands of their boss, John Gage, UO director of composition. I was also told that personal notes and union literature were taken from instructor offices, and at least one instructor I talked to is removing all remaining AFT literature from her office. I was also told that Gage and English Department chair Paul Armstrong attempted to stop at least one instructor promotion.

The day before the promotion committee met in early 1988, the instructor asked to see her personnel file and then copied everything in that file. She found nothing related to union activity, but when the committee met, John Gage pulled union documents from the file. Gage had allegedly kept secret files on union activists, something he also denied when I interviewed him. According to a letter written by the instructor's attorney, what Gage had done was "an illegal insertion" (a violation of ORS 243.672) of union materials into a personnel file to stop a promotion. Denial of promotion would have meant automatic nonrenewal of contract for the instructor. She would have been fired though it's against the law to discharge an employee for union organizing.

The instructor had grounds for a major law suit but decided that if she wanted to stay in teaching, she'd better not cause trouble. She fought back just hard enough to get the promotion, but got it only after Paul Armstrong gave her a left-handed recommendation, agreeing with John Gage that she was "unsupervisable." An odd comment given that instructors are hired as independent professionals needing no direct supervision. The instructor is now in the process of filing a formal grievance.

I described the case to Norman Wessells without mentioning names because many instructors had and have a very real concern about being fired for talking to me. The provost said that placing union materials in a personnel file to stop a promotion was "utterly inappropriate and improper. That kind of retribution has no place at a place like this."

*

The way to stop unions on campus, said an attorney in *The Chronicle of Higher Education* who advises university administrators on stopping unions from forming, is to remove conditions that lead to them. Such as? Lack of communication between management and workers, favoritism, poor wages, benefits, and working conditions. One source told me that if the University of Oregon had only treated instructors better, the effort to form a union never would have happened in the first place. Reality, however, is otherwise. Because using up teachers and busting their unions became the favorite management tool of the '80s for keeping labor cheap, removing conditions that led to unions only happened where unions existed--in California, for instance, where the AFT exercised serious political influence and pushed for reform.

In March of 1989, the California Assembly Joint Committee for Review of the Master Plan for Higher Education, chaired by John Vasconcellos, published the final report on California's entire public higher education system, including the University of California and California State University. "Absolutely central to any hope for quality undergraduate education must be an uncompromising commitment to excellence in undergraduate teaching," the report said. "And we hear evidence aplenty that not all serious researchers are devoted to teaching. Indeed, we know that universities create research positions explicitly designed to include little teaching, and other 'teaching' positions are made more attractive to candidates on the basis of reducing the teaching to a minimum."

The committee recommended that the state university governing boards make teaching as important as research and "ensure that teaching is of major importance" in faculty evaluation. The committee ordered the governing boards to evaluate the use of part-time teachers and to report on that evaluation to the California Assembly in 1990.

Norman Wessells arrived a year ago from Stanford University, which isn't part of the California state higher ed system. But Wessells was hired to run Oregon's largest public university, so it's safe to assume he knows something about tax-supported universities in California, a state that sets national trends in higher ed. When I mentioned California reform during the interview, he nodded politely and said nothing, but he is going to study the instructor problem.

Myles Brand and Norman Wessells met with Paul Armstrong, John Gage, and four instructors on November 28, 1989. Brand assured instructors that he'd look into the salary question. Wessells told me in late December that he and his senior vice-provost, Gerry Kissler, newly arrived from UCLA, would examine the "structure" of the University of Oregon instructor position after Christmas. The study would be completed, he hoped, by the end of March, 1990.

On January 11, 1990, Governor Goldschmidt told University of Oregon faculty he'd ask the legislature for

$50 million to improve faculty salaries. The state, he said, must take "dramatic measures" to go after highly ranked professors and to keep the best teachers from leaving. "You are wanted," he said, "You are needed."

First published in What's Happening, *22 Feb. 1990: 4.*

SNOBS

Jean Anderson

Darrin is sitting off to the side, on the floor. Not under the skylight in the public library's waiting area. Not on one of the shiny wooden benches scattered among the delicate indoor trees, but here in the shadows next to the tray filled with brochures. He's waiting to be picked up after school where she told him to wait, yes, but here he can see his mother before she sees him. Here he can think, which he needs to do; maybe figure out how to tell her. And there she is suddenly, too soon. Though late as always of course, ten minutes late, wearing her new used parka and looking breathless --red-cheeked, harried, her face serious and somber as always while she struggles through the big glass double doors with her stack of books and the records she's returning.

He guesses his mother must be the only woman left in the world who still checks out--and listens to, actually *plays*—the library's ancient phonograph records. Poets reading their own poems, black disks she spins in her classes and also listens to herself, frozen in place sometimes while she washes the dishes at night, listening before she begins grading papers. On the few nights when she's not teaching, that is.

"Other teachers buy tapes, Mom." He'd told her that about a month ago. Because he saw the tapes in a catalog she got in the mail: *Poets Speak.* But she said no of course; tapes would be too expensive, that was the reason; he knew it even though she didn't say it. *Ochen dorogova--very* expensive, in Russian. She's trying to learn that from the big, old shiny-black records too: Russian, "for Siberian visitors, dear," an interest she's added since he lived with her last, a year ago.

"The library's recordings are perfectly good, Darrin," she'd said last month, turning the cheap paper catalog around in her hands. She was trying hard not to frown; he could tell.

"Wouldn't the world be a better place if we all shared things, honey? If we used up what we have that's still good before we rush out to buy new?"

She even carries his old portable record player to her classes, the one his grandparents gave him for Christmas when he was only a baby. She doesn't always have time to drive up to the campus, she says, find parking and so on, and pick up a phonograph--often broken anyway --from the audio-visual room, then repeat the entire process to return it on time. Which seems to him no reason at all. No reason for an adult to carry a child's tiny portable record player covered with red and yellow beach-ball stuff like wallpaper. Besides, he knows she also doesn't allow herself to "waste gas," since she most often teaches not on campus but in town, or else out on the military base. Which--"wasting gas"--really means, again, he knows it, just money: *ochen dorogova.*

Darrin sighs, grits his teeth, squeezes his eyes closed for a minute before he stands up and walks toward her, and he's not quite dragging his backpack. He's being careful about that. They've already quarreled several times since he arrived from Juneau about his habit of dragging things. But why does she always make him *feel* like dragging things? Even his own feet? That's the real question as far as he's concerned. *Why?* Why is *his* mother the only woman he knows who buys used coats that look nearly as bad as the one she's just worn out?

"Oh, honey," she says, seeing him at last, "give me a hand, will you? Grab these records before I drop them--?"

And one of her students--of course--is rushing up to them from some place. Popping out of the woodwork is what Dad would call it: "Here, Doctor Taylor. Let me help." The student is hush-voiced as they always are around his mother, reverent, like somebody breathlessly saying a prayer they've worked hard to memorize. So Darrin only grabs a few of the books, while the student--who has long dirty hair and a bad case of acne, as the hushed-voiced ones always do seem to have, either or both--takes the records. He hates it when they call her "Doctor Taylor." Because most of the time she stops right then, on the spot, and corrects them, blocking the path and so on, telling them that her dissertation isn't quite complete.

Not saying that she can't afford to leave Fairbanks and go back Outside to work on it; maybe never will be able to afford to go back, ever, which he knows is the truth--saying only that she isn't really Doctor Taylor yet. Just yet. That's how she always puts it: "Just yet."

The same when they say "Professor." She's actually an adjunct faculty member, a lecturer in the department, she tells them, her voice so achingly precise. Not a professor: *"Ms. Taylor will do just fine."* He hates the way she smiles when she says it, her face so damned pure, glowing, almost radiant--beatific, he thinks that's the word; he came across it once in one of her dictionaries. As if "being paid *nothing* to teach class after class, year after year," which he heard her sobbing about, crying into the telephone to his grandmother one day just last week, saying: "It's just--*so wrong,* Mom. So abusive. Demeaning. Hurtful--" Well, smiling as if all that is exactly the thing she's dreamed of and longed for forever while she talks with one of her students.

But she doesn't say any of it this time.

"Rodrigo, I'd like you to meet my son Darrin." She says that to the student instead. And Darrin nods politely, trying not to let his eyes wander over the student's strange-looking clothes and even more puzzling yellowish skin while his mind is bouncing the fact of the odd-sounding name like a basketball added to all the rest: Native American? But what--? Tlinget? Asian and African maybe? But then why Rodrigo? Maybe Filipino--? Surely not a Siberian--?

"Rodrigo is a chess player too, Darrin," she's saying. And Darrin is suddenly ashamed of himself. Ashamed of his own clunky and uncontrolled mind--a racist's mind? His thinking probably proves that he's at least some kind of major snob-in-training. Because snobs are what his mother hates most. He doesn't know how many times he's heard her proclaim it, thousands probably. And he *does* agree in a way. Totally maybe. But--face it--he does *not* want to be forced into playing chess with this head-bobbing person who reminds him of a bookend in his grandparents' bedroom in Juneau. Good God, no!

"Neat," he says instead, trying to smile at the student, hoping with a splash of her own phrasing to please his mother for once.   Rodrigo is smiling back painfully.

The bookend is what's left of a pair, Gramma's told him--a little ceramic man who looks as if he's some pale American version of an oriental, some China-boy thought up by an occidental.   The tiny ceramic head sways constantly, bobbing up and down anytime anybody gets anywhere near the bookend.   He can't imagine two of them, ever.   He thinks somebody probably broke the other one to put it out of its misery--and now here's this real-live Rodrigo, still bobbing his head.

It's all too much, suddenly: his mother trying to learn Russian from the library's old records, even borrowing his wornout record player to play them. Then this shabby student. And the fact that he can't go to the dentist this year, not once, *will not,* will *not* tell his mother about his new aching cavity, since he knows that she has no medical coverage. He'll suffer silently and wait till next year, with Dad, when he'll be covered again.

And of course he won't tell her what he's been thinking at all. He *won't* dammit, *will not* tell her that he's homesick. That he wants to go back to Dad this year again--that he'd rather be back home with Dad and his new family. "Home"--that's how he's begun to think of it. No, he'll tough it out this year, here, in the junior high he hates, watching TV alone at night most nights while she's out teaching, trying to focus on his homework in the shabby little living room where she sleeps on the couch so he can have her bedroom. Listening to those scratchy Russian records, to poets nobody ever heard of intoning their odd-sounding words. Riding in her wornout Honda and hoping it won't break down or drift off into a snowbank. Thinking about eating more than doing it, since he knows how little money she has. Thinking about being laid back, cozy, sprawled in the big easy chair in front of the big TV at Dad's, eating popcorn, staring into the fireplace, drinking juice or pop, pigging out, joking with his half-brother--next year.

Being an ordinary American again, with parents who have real jobs that pay real money. Parents who let you buy new clothes rather than garage-sale specials. Who let you go to a movie rather than always borrowing old ones--"classics"--from the library--or to the dentist. Because all that *is* what he wants; he sees it now. To be a *real* American, a snob, at Dad's.

How can he tell her that here it is only October and already he'd rather be there? That he'd rather be back in Juneau with Dad and his new family? Well, he won't. Dammit, of course he won't. Instead he'll keep on doing what he's doing--just as she will. Walking stiffly ahead carrying borrowed books. Walking behind this weird-looking kid called Rodrigo who's probably only one of the eighty or so she's teaching English classes to this semester for five dollars an hour, some of them probably far worse off than this.

He'll keep right on, putting one foot in front of the other, smiling falsely and pretending not to be a snob; saying it again, slightly louder: "Chess, huh? Neat."

JOURNAL ENTRY 5/13/93

Kat Snider Blackbird

A good thing to do now would be to go to bed.
Tomorrow will be filled with wonderful new
challenges and opportunities to do things
that make the world more beautiful.

Could go to bed now, got a busy day tomorrow.
Gotta meet with Dr. Heathcliff,
make sure I look like an intelligent,
vibrant, somewhat subdued, mature,
like--grown up--you know,
so I can maybe get an appointment
for a Lectureship.

Yes, this is a political poem.
I write poems.
And I teach poetry, or, shall we say,
Creative Writing, at the University.
I am a *master* of *art,*
I teach very well.
I have to prove this tomorrow morning,
to Dr. Heathcliff,

so maybe he'll give me
a Lectureship.

Of course they'll probably hire a Ph.D.

See, if I got a Lectureship,
I would more or less be guaranteed
three classes in the fall and four in the spring,
or *four* in the fall and three in the spring,
AND, I'd get 2,000 dollars per course
instead of 1800 per course, that's for
the lower division courses--for the
upper division courses I'd get
2200 or maybe even 2300 per course.
So I'd be teaching seven courses
instead of four, and I'd be making
possibly even fourteen thousand dollars
a year instead of the seventy-two hundred
I make now. Wow.

There's still no health insurance or
anything like that but it would be a pretty
sure thing I'd get renewed each semester,
I mean not *100%* for sure, but you'd
have a better chance, although you never know.

Yes, tomorrow, I will see Dr. Heathcliff.
I probably won't go into my ideas
about revolution from within--
won't do anything too dramatic
like get on my knees and beg for money
so I can teach and get some

sleep already, won't beg him
to let me teach because I am a brilliant teacher
or that he give me money because I have
fifty nine dollars to my name--

Well, that's not *100%* true, I *do* still have
the house and I *could* sell it--
and I do have a fairly nice car my father *did*
buy for me--And, *"my kid needs braces"*
isn't going to raise a lot of sympathy
in anyone who reads The New York Times,
I mean after all, times are hard,
what can we do.

Yes, I went to the *Education Celebration*
at my daughter's elementary school last night.
There was nothing really *wrong* with it
but I'd just like to *casually* suggest
that the school, built in 1949 out of red
and orange and burgundy bricks looks *somewhat*
like a penitentiary and the straight
halls and the amazing bells and the way
the children line up and the way
the teachers dress and do strange things
with their lips--

Dr. Heathcliff? The freshmen can't write.
They know no grammar, and there is no division
for this, upper or lower, it's too late
to go that far back--and I am telling you
I can teach them to write and I am begging you
to let me, and they will say that I am

the best teacher they've ever had
and thank *God* for me, and they will be
writers and they will tell their stories
because their stories *need* to be told,
I tell you they *need* to be told--

And you must give me money.
And health insurance.
And *job security*
so I can say to my students,
on the first day of class, darlings,
let me tell you a story.
When I was your age,
my first semester of college,
homesick,
boy back home,
afraid of the cool girl in the dorm room next to mine
who had the coolest posters and the coolest stereo
with huge speakers and played Led Zeppelin loud,
when I had no idea what to *major* in, and had
eighteen hours of L.E.R.'s and one of them
was Introduction to Astronomy,
well.

When I heard the learn'd astronomer,
When the proofs, the figures, were arranged in columns
    before me,
When I was shown the charts and diagrams, to add, divide,
    and measure them,
When I sitting heard the astronomer where he lectured
    with much applause in the lecture-room,
How soon unaccountable I became tired and sick,

Till rising and gliding out I wander'd off by myself,
In the mystical moist night-air, and from time to time,
Look'd up in perfect silence at the stars.

And then, Dr. Heathcliff, learning begins.
The hungry are fed.

The needy are clothed and sheltered.
The maniacs still and begin to hear
the song of a bird, the grasses to bow down
in the breeze and rise again,
and then, there is
peace on earth,
and then,
learning begins.

I'm going to bed now.
Goodnight.
Sweet dreams.

No, you're fired.

Or maybe,
My lawyer will contact your lawyer.

I tell you I can teach!
You'd be nuts not to hire me!

I want special topics courses.
Literature, Emily Dickinson,
and
Creative Writing

and
Poetry,
I want an auditorium with a stage
and a sound system
and a sound man,
two of them,
and lights,
two people working the lights.

I want appointees from the
Theatre Department,
the English Department,
the Foreign Language Departments.
Sociology, Anthropology,
Psychology, Biology, Geography,
Geology, Chemistry, Biochemistry,
Psychology, Pharmacology,
Biological Anthropology,
Cellular and Molecular Biology,
Zoology, Ecology, Botany, Art.

Philosophy.
Nursing.
Speech Pathology and Audiology.
Technology.
Criminal Justice Studies.
Family and Consumer Studies.
Classical Studies.
Architecture and Environmental Design.

Political Science
and Government, International

Relations, Physics,
Physical Education,
Recreation.
Dance.

I want students on my staff
and I want faculty on my staff
and I want adjunct faculty on my staff
and I want lecturers, performers, researchers.

Theory and composition.
Orchestration.
Musicology.
Ethnomusicology.
Conducting.

Computer Science.
Mathematical Science.
Library Science.

Journalism and Mass Communications.
Photography.
News.

History.

Department of Rehabilitation Counseling and Training.
School Counseling Department.
Speech Communication.

Outdoor Education.
Ceramics. Jewelry making.

Organic Gardening.

I want them to be on call.
They will do what I say.
Students, and their parents,
will have to sign a waiver
before entering the hall
releasing me and the university
of any responsibility.
Because in this class
we are going to do things.
We will be doing things.

Everyone will have to have
complete faith in my ability
to teach--
Emily Dickinson, for example.
A special topics course: Emily on Consciousness.

It's hard to explain in words why I am a great teacher
and why I deserve a job.
I want you to come observe my teaching.
But I want you to come on the first day
and stay throughout.
I don't *want* you to just drop in,
although you may do that.
Come any time.

I want $60,000 a year,
tenure, and health insurance,
and a tuition fee waiver
for my kids,

and dental insurance
that covers orthodontia.

Sign here,

_____

T. Heathcliff
5/14/93

OPEN LETTER TO NEW (AND USED) SCHOLARS--CATS IN THE AIR, DOGS IN THE RAIN

Cayle

The hardest part about this business is the limbo, the deracination in between appointments. You've done the research universities, little colleges, business schools, public and private schools, even secretarial schools, the tutoring, editing, proofreading medical texthooks, and other odd jobs. If you're lucky, you live in that increasing chasm between academic worlds: to your students you're one of the Authorities, but to the tenured faculty you're one of the large and mobile rabble of gypsy scholars. You have a schedule that would kill Atilla the Hun. In your six free hours a week you commute to a school that is out-of-state, across the state, or in another county where the pay is *so low* that you wish it were *duo*. Then you arrive like a quasi-Emissary of High Culture, Peace Corps Volunteer, Cog in Somebody Else's Machine, and/or Grammar Police (knowing in painful detail how prescriptive grammarians for the last two centuries wanted to sort the middle class out from the lower ones). Your students write sentences like Tristan Tzara, Samuel Beckett, and Gertrude Stein--all at once--but they don't know Dada from mama, the Absurd from the ridiculous, or automatic writing from automatic reading. (Order your RONCO Automatic Interpreting Reader for the Higher Education Anomie Disabled. . . . Just Dial 1-800-A-I-R-H-E-A-D. It reads, interprets, and grades student essays all in one easy to follow state of sociopathic apathy. Don't resort to major pharmaceuticals when you get that glazed absence of attention-span feeling. Theory Models limited--out of state deconstructions void where they apply.)

But seriously, if you could wake up, you'd be outraged. You thought nothing could be better than this--stepping into the classroom full of eager faces. They almost make up for the commute, the subway track fires, the shuttle bus breakdowns, the strangers smashed against you breathing on the side of your head. They almost make up for the upscale waitress-level wages, except waitresses get paid more than three times a semester. They almost make up for the BUREAUCRACY (the only religious affiliation that makes you tremble with fear), for around the block your fellow adjuncts in line wind mysteriously into office complex mazes for privileges as big as a parking sticker which isn't even free. They almost make up for the bomb scares that evacuate the classrooms on the day of final exams. . . . And yet, and yet, and yet--because of those faces, you miss the place . . . .

It is still a place that still believes itself to be a myth, a place where the great have come and gone (with salaries literally hundreds of times greater than yours). And the most horrific epiphany is seeing someone younger and less experienced than yourself show up like a raw recruit. She could have been a beautiful friend in another world, but it's too late. You try to throw her a life-line, to warn her about the lecherous chairperson, to tell her about the merciless voluntary committee chores, to alert her to the vexation of dreams portioned out in teaspoon-sized grants, fellowships and awards, dreams that will be deferred. There in that tiny almost-office, that is, almost enough room to speak freely, you see that she cannot believe you. The country she comes from has no poor professors--she will not believe what she sees. You wish you could repatriate yourself to her country of inexperience, but Limbo is an ecumenical phenomenon. In it, we're like cats in the air, dogs in the rain.

COMP DOG

Barry Greer

Jean Roberts (not her real name) will retire at the end of the 1989-1990 academic year from one of Oregon's largest tax-supported universities. She'll get a $500-a-month pension after 25 years of service in the state system. "I got to thinking," she told me, "that I started teaching in 1964 and that if I were to characterize my teaching experience, it would have to be a history of exploitation, manipulation, and double-talk."

Jean's department chair tried to force her out of her job two years short of retirement because she'd been teaching at the university for six years. Her job and the pittance of a pension were saved when a tenured professor went to the chair and threatened to go public if Jean were fired.

She described her first teaching job in Portland as a padded cell. "I was a product of the 50s," she said, when "women were told that if they were cooperative and good and hard working and didn't make any trouble, didn't rock the boat, weren't political, and smiled a lot, that they would succeed. . . . I was rewarded by being hired term to term."

She quoted from a 1975 letter she received after teaching 11 years. "It is my task to inform you about DC writing classes, for you may be wondering whether you are teaching fall term. The answer, unfortunately, is no." Such letters had one of three standard excuses for firing an instructor: change in personnel policy, drop in enrollment, lack of funding.

Even the letters telling her she had a job were insulting. A 1976 notification of hire told her "that since your appointment is related to enrollment, I am obligated to say that we reserve the right to cancel."

In 1977, Jean said, "I was told that my teaching load did not come up to .5 FTE [Full Time Equivalent] and therefore I would be dropped from Kaiser [health insurance plan]. My contracts documented that I taught at least three classes per term, and often one or two summer school classes. The university also stopped PERS [Public Employment Retirement System] for me: no retirement, no pension. When I asked about it they said, well the reason you are less than .5 FTE, even though you teach three courses a term, is that you do not serve on any committees. Well, I said, I would be very happy to serve on committees, and they told me I could not serve on committees unless I had a .5 appointment."

Nor could she accumulate any seniority teaching at the first university. "What happened was that I was told I had been laid off a term, and they had the rules written so that an instructor had to have taught so many years consecutively without interruption to gain seniority." She was laid off because of a drop in enrollment, or so she was told.

Once she asked her department chair how she was doing as a teacher because no evaluation system existed at the time. She was told she "was a professional," but then, Jean said, "I complained a little bit about the low salary and I was told that I was an auxiliary income and I was paid always with the idea in mind that there was a major breadwinner somewhere out there supporting me, and that's how they rationalized the low pay."

But the cell was padded in the first position. In spite of the low pay and Orwellian personnel rules, Jean felt at home because she was still married to a tenured faculty member and because teaching was a respected part of the job for all faculty members, part-time or full-time, tenured or not.

Jean described her treatment at the university she's now retiring from as social Darwinism. "I have told some of my friends who are Jewish teachers here that I feel just as threatened as they do because I am a gypsy and the showers loomed in my future just as much as in theirs. I called this place Dachau West when I came here and that's my nickname for this place."

"I think I'd have either done myself in or had a nervous breakdown," Jean said, if she hadn't had solid self-respect. When I asked her how she would describe the attitude of her current department chair toward instructors, she said without a half-second hesitation, "Contempt. Absolute contempt." Her chair lied to her constantly. "Always the downside, always the warning, always the cuts, always what's going wrong, always the shortness of the budget, and so, you know, you're supposed to be grateful there is any kind of job at all. Absolute total doublespeak. Up is down. Left is right. Black is white."

"In other words, during 24 years of teaching, I had seven years of benefits and most of the earnings of my time here where I've had benefits, have been under $12,000 a year."

Originally published in What's Happening *22 Feb. 1990: 5.*

EDUCATING JOSHUA

Barry Greer

I had the opportunity to teach the governor's son, Joshua Goldschmidt, at Oregon State University. I wish I hadn't. Josh got short changed, and given the governor's concern as a parent and taxpayer for education, I thought he'd like to know why each student in a typical introductory required writing course at one of Oregon's two largest tax-supported universities gets little for his or her literacy dollar.

Before giving specifics, I need to explain how the OSU English Department works. I wouldn't want to leave the impression that administrative stupefaction about teaching students basic writing skills is any different on the Corvallis campus now than it has been for the last 40 years. Classes have always been crowded. Low pay, no job security, and pariah status have been and remain the norm for writing instructors.

Those conditions exist because literacy at Oregon State is seen as reading only, as taking a few literature courses. A quick check of the *Random House College Dictionary* reveals that literacy is "the ability to read and write." Being able to write clear prose is an essential survival skill during and after college. Yet writing courses have about the same status at OSU as slug roping. Some instructors are hired a term at a time. Some are hired for nine months and let go. A favored few are hired arbitrarily from one year to the next. But when the budget is cut, instructors get axed first. And rarely, if ever, is a writing instructor promoted.

Only two instructors to my knowledge moved up to professor in the English Department. By winning the National Book Award, Bernard Malamud embarrassed Oregon State into promoting him from instructor to associate professor. Malamud, who went on to win a second National and a Pulitzer Prize, left OSU in 1961 and couldn't be lured back. Daniel Armstrong, a film scholar who has taught business writing in the OSU English Department for over a decade, was once promoted to assistant professor. For one year. Then demoted to instructor the next year at starting pay. In 1988 he received the Burlington Northern Foundation Faculty Achievement Award for outstanding university teaching.

He's still an instructor.

The 12-course-a-year teaching load has changed little from the day Malamud began teaching in 1949, while full-time teaching at the University of Oregon for writing instructors has dropped to 10 courses. John Gage, UO director of composition, once asked me with genuine curiosity and a touch of disbelief how anyone could teach four college courses in one term.

My answer: "You can't."

With 27 students per class, OSU writing instructors teach 324 students a year, 84 more than recommended in 1987 by the National Council of Teachers of English. "In sections larger than 20, teachers cannot possibly give student writing the immediate and individual response necessary for growth and improvement."

But why not mass lecture sections like other college courses? "Everyone recognizes," said Wayne Booth, a leading expert on college composition who teaches at the

University of Chicago, "that for all other technical skills individual attention is needed. Yet for this, the most delicate of all skills, the one requiring the most subtle interrelationships of training, character, and experience, we fling students and teachers into hopelessly impersonal patterns." Twenty-five years ago Booth recommended three classes per term, 15 students per class, for each teacher.

In 1987, two consultants from the Council of Writing Program Administrators (WPA), Seattle University professor John C. Bean and Northern Michigan University professor Mark Smith, evaluated the OSU composition program. "Blind evolution," they noted in their report, "seems to explain the current anomalous situation at OSU--a literature program that emulates a major research university and a composition program that emulates a large, underfunded community college." One consequence is instructor discontent. "Most instructors we talked to felt extremely alientated from Oregon State University and angry towards everyone involved in the writing program--the administration, the coordinators, the tenured facility members . . . ." Why? "The reasons cited for this hostility were low pay, lack of job security, heavy teaching load, lack of variety in teaching assignments, lack of recognition of their contributions, and the recently instituted evaluation system."

Dale Sloat, founder and former head of the University of Oregon Linguistic Department, joined the OSU English Department in 1986 as an instructor. Once, in disgust, he told me that OSU instructors were no more than "grading machines." After two years, Sloat resigned.

Josh Goldschmidt and the other students knew none of this, of course, when they registered for freshmen comp. Josh was a typical American college student, meaning he came to college with poor writing skills and will most likely graduate with poor skills. He's a good kid, though, and added humor to a class full of skittish first term freshmen.

The term I taught Josh, I had the usual hundred or so students to teach during a 50 hour week. I spent 12 of those 50 in class. I grade two sets of papers a week, at minimum, each set taking six to eight hours to complete. Preparation, if I want to do more than dust off the same old notes each term, takes another 10 hours a week. Which leaves me with 12 hours to give individual attention to each of the hundred, or 7.2 minutes per student.

Besides teaching, I worked with a professor who was writing a composition texthook. She needed two instructors to use the draft in a class, to keep notes on use, and to meet with her to discuss the project. I needed the money. St. Martin's Press, the professor's publisher, paid me $200 for helping with the texthook.

I was also writing. Though I'm not required to practice what I teach, I do anyway, and publications improve my vita for perpetual job hunting--the consequence of constant termination anxiety. For instance, two instructors hired for spring term, 1987, were not rehired for fall 1988. A third instructor, Andrea Lerner, was told she would have work through winter term of 1988, but not after. Lerner is a Reed-Stanford graduate and a published poet.

Malamud was the rule, not the exception.

Nick Catuccio, a Columbia graduate, gone after a year. Bonnie Lund, a screen writer, gone after a year. Beth Camp, co-author of a business text and the instructor who introduced computer-aided writing to the OSU English Department, gone after a year. Gordon Mennenga, graduate of the University of Iowa creative writing program (the finest in the country) and writer for National Public Radio's *A Prairie Home Companion,* gone after one term. Ruth Gidian, poet and now an editor at *Nonhwest Review,* among the best literary quarterlies in the country, gone after one term. Steven Sher, author of four poetry books, gone.

According to the WPA consultants, "While it is not unusual to find, especially at a state university, that much of the composition teaching is done by non-tenure-line faculty, it is unusual to find so many instructors with superior professional credentials." They need them; the vita always has to be ready for the mail.

But, to be fair, improvements have been made at Oregon State to assure literacy means reading and writing.

1) The English Department remodeled the second floor Moreland Hall student lounge and named it after Bernard Malamud.

2) Four instructors (none of them me) with doctorates--two male, two female--remained instructors while the English Department hired Dr. Sandra Spanier, the wife of the incoming provost, as an assistant professor. A position was created for her, no job search was conducted, none of the usual hiring procedures followed. According to the *Barometer,* the OSU campus

newspaper, the Spanier hire clearly violated university affirmative action guidelines. To welcome Professor Spanier, a faculty member stuffed mail boxes with this J. R. Ewing quote: "Once you get past integrity, the rest is a piece of cake."

3) The provost demonstrated his sensitivity to the matter by ordering reduced teaching loads for "productive" (those who publish, including his wife) literature professors. A reduced teaching load encouraged lit profs to write. But writing instructors continued to be told they were hired "to teach." Not to write.

4) The American Federation of Teachers' 1987 attempt to organize research assistant/instructor unions at the University of Oregon and Oregon State University was stopped cold by an inexplicable Employment Relations Board decision to deny bargaining rights.

5) In October 1988 the College of Liberal Arts dean announced that instructors would have the opportunity to achieve tenure and the rank of senior instructor. At the same time he said bluntly that few instructors would be chosen, that most had better start looking for work. English Department chair Bob Frank plans to chop the number to four full-time instructors by 1990, from 13 in 1987-1988, 20 in 1986-1987. The number of courses remains the same. They'll be taught by graduate assistants, mostly women, earning sub-poverty wages.

6) Sandra Spanier was granted tenure in 1989.

It'd be nice to say that the problem is only an OSU problem, that if Josh has gone to the University of Oregon, Southern Oregon, or Eastern Oregon he would have gotten more for his literacy dollar. But according to M. Elizabeth Wallace, an expert on the neglect of basic writing in higher education, the problem exists in all of Oregon's state colleges and universities.

Recently I had to help an OSU honors student with her thesis. She didn't know how to organize it. When I taught at the University of Oregon, a business student frantically came into my office one day with a folder full of disheveled papers. She'd completed all her work for her Ph.D. but couldn't write the dissertation. She didn't know how to organize it.

Every 18-year-old transfer student from Great Britain I've taught writes superbly organized, clearly written essays.

Maybe it's time to put a little of that lottery money into low tech, into keeping skilled writers in higher education, skilled writers who teach what they do best. Engineers teach engineering, biologists teach biology, philosophers teach philosophy, musicians teach music, artists teach art, but a university writing instructor is the only teacher who doesn't have to practice what he or she teaches, who is discouraged from doing so by a system of blind neglect.

I'm doing what the dean told me to do. I'm leaving OSU the first chance I get. I'm fed up with cheating students out of their hard-earned literacy dollars.

First printed in What's Happening *on 16 Nov. 1989.*

THE ONLY GOOD WRITER
IS A DEAD WRITER

Barry Greer

Bernard Malamud's novel, *The Assistant,* was
required reading during my senior year in high school in
1963-1964. It was the first time life and literature
merged for me. Frank Alpine lived in my mind--Alpine
the outsider, the goy finding redemption in love and
literature and Judaism. But it was more than adolescent
fantasy. *The Assistant* connected me to life on Vera
Avenue in Cincinnati, Ohio where we had the only tree
at Christmas, where I was as conscious of Passover as I
was of Easter, where my father would chat on the
sidewalk with Mr. Zeff, a neighbor who had a
concentration camp number tattoo on his forearm. *The
Assistant* evoked memories of Michael Tannenbaum's
barmitzvah, of hearing him read from the Torah for the
first time in synagogue. Mike was the kid I'd played
ball and skated with when we lived in Lynn,
Massachusetts. His mother had given me my first taste
of matzo in the third floor kitchen of the three decker
they lived in across the street from our house. Matzo
tasted like a saltless soda cracker and offered me some
vague contact with Jewish history, the same contact I
felt when I touched the Tannenbaum mezuzah just like
Mike did when he left by the kitchen door to go down
the back stairway.

So, yes, I knew that Judaism was something more than reading the Old Testament on the Sabbath. Mike and Mr. Zeff and Bernard Malamud and his characters were all part of a long and distant history as well as part of the recent horror of the Holocaust.

But not until 1980, not until I went to graduate school at the University of Oregon did I know of Malamud's academic novel, *A New Life*, and learn that Malamud had arrived in Oregon in 1949 to teach at Oregon State College and had left in 1961 just before *A New Life* was published and OSC became OSU. One professor during my first term mentioned it in passing as he lectured on *The Magic Barrel*. He smiled and said that people were still guessing which characters in *A New Life* were based on which faculty members at Oregon State. After that comment, I had to read *A New Life*. Not because I sought gossip about the inanities of academic life, but because Malamud was a literary hero who had lived not forty miles from where I sat in Eugene. In Corvallis, Oregon, a backwater college town, he'd written his way to the pinnacle of American letters. But because I knew by then as a graduate student that serious fiction was written for analysis, I did not react to *A New Life* as I did to *The Assistant*. Instead I placed it in all the correct canonical categories: academic farce, schlemiel story, tragicomedy. The censorship theme I ignored. It was just so much furniture, I figured, in an existential setting, a backdrop for Sy Levin, another Malamud character seeking redemption through love. Besides, McCarthyism was dead and gone.

It was not until 1984 that I began to learn the consequences of disconnecting literature from life to gain analytical distance from something called a text. As Malamud was reading his memoirs for the Bennington College Ben Belitt lecture series in October of 1984, describing how he "seized the opportunity" to leave Oregon, I was scrambling to survive my first term as a full-time writing instructor at Oregon State University in Corvallis. For the next seven years I walked the dim, worn Moreland Hall corridors thinking that Malamud had taught where I was teaching. Not in the same building. Moreland was the old Forestry building that housed the English Department after the building where Malamud had once graded papers had been torn down. Maybe to raze his memory, because there was nothing in Moreland to indicate Malamud had ever been in Oregon. Until Malamud died in 1986, the English Department put nothing on the walls to celebrate or even to hint that for a dozen years it was the place where one of the greatest voices in 20th Centnry American literature taught and wrote. Yes, Malamud returned to visit OSU. Yes, he stayed in touch with Oregon friends. And yes, OSU hosted a 1975 conference on Malamud's fiction. But even then recognition seemed backhanded. The English Department chair at the time said Malamud was "the most distinguished faculty member" ever to teach at OSU. But the comment had a hollow ring to it. Malamud wrote *The Natural, The Assistant,* and *The Magic Barrel* while he was in Oregon. He won a *Partisan* Review-Rockefeller grant, the Daroff Memorial Award, a National Institute of Arts and Letters award, and the National Book Award while he was in Oregon. But the OSU English Department never promoted him past associate professor. While I was at OSU, a literature professor with one book could get promoted to associate professor, and a second book meant promotion to full professor. It took fourteen years, a second National, and a Pulitzer Prize before OSU organized one little conference on its "most distinguished faculty member." Maybe the chair spoke closer to the truth when he said that the conference would transform a "pain in the ass" into a "cultural monument," meaning that the conference would belatedly change the OSU attitude toward Malamud. But by 1975, of course, the pain in the ass needed no transformation.

Even after his death, the OSU English Department offered only begrudging respect to the Brooklyn Jew. OSU put a photo of the dead pain in the ass on the wall of a small, second floor Moreland Hall student lounge. Below the photo, in a locked glass case, were a few hard cover editions of Malamud fiction and his letter of application for the job of writing instructor, a letter that mentioned he was writing a novel with the working title of *The Light Sleeper.* Below that case were samples of OSU literature faculty scholarship. That was it.

That and an *apologia* on OSU's treatment of Malamud written by Oregon State University assistant professor Suzanne Clark, which was published by *The American Scholar* in 1990. Clark acknowledged the anti-Semitism Malamud faced, but claimed Malamud had been a progressive influence on the OSU English Department even though he left it just before having a novel published that was anything but a flattering reflection on the place, a novel nobody in the Department knew about until Malamud was safely on the other side of the continent.

Still, Clark did her best to make it appear as if things had changed because of Malamud. She wrote that by "1961, when Malamud left, a number of the 'young Turks' at Oregon State were excited about writing, literature, and teaching the liberal arts. Malamud encouraged their rebellion against the older regime. Many of them saw *A New Life,* in fact, as a manifesto in favor of their cause." Malamud, Clark added, once even came to the defense of an instructor who was nearly fired.

But little had really changed at Oregon State during the twenty-three years between Malamud's exit and the day I walked onto campus. The OSU English Department was still modeled after the cast system built at Harvard by Francis Child, who invented literary study in 1876 to escape the grading of student compositions. At OSU literature scholarship dominated, rhetoric and composition were poor relations, and those who dirtied their hands teaching writing to undergraduates were reminded that they were lucky to have a job. Just as Malamud was, just as Sy Levin was in *A New Life,* I was assigned four writing courses each term. I wasn't allowed to teach literature, because instructors, with or without a PhD, were hired to teach writing and nothing but writing. The number of students I taught was the same number Malamud and Sy Levin taught, a number that increased by the time I left. Just as Malamud and Levin did, I worked under the constant threat of having my contract canceled. I was paid what a starting high school teacher earned, and with no hope of ever doing better. Literature professors taught one course fewer a term, two courses fewer by the time I left, at pay fifty to one hundred percent more than what instructors earned, pay that increased at three times their rate.

I worked day to day with subtle and not so subtle reminders (if the pay weren't enough) that I was a second class citizen in the English Department. The literature faculty called those who taught composition "comp dogs." Dogs controlled no committee, earned no sabbatical, and even had to fight to get parental leave for the birth of a child. I had to go all the way to a central administration official to get the English chair to grant me leave for the 1989 birth of my daughter. And the only two serious attempts at English Department reform were squashed flat in 1987. A consultant's report that called the OSU writing program no better than that of a poor community college was buried and forgotten. An attempt by the AFT to organize instructors at the University of Oregon and OSU was stopped by a backdoor political deal.

But my attitude was never one of acceptance. Because I knew the system was corrupt never meant I had to like the system any more than Malamud did. Malamud faced anti-Semitism at OSU, but he kept the job because it gave him the time to write. Keeping the job, however, didn't mean he had to keep his mouth shut about working conditions. And he didn't. My job paid me enough to get by, gave me an office, a library card, and time to write. That's why I took the job. That and the idea that teaching writing was important.

So I refused to accept the status quo and, like Malamud, wrote what I wanted to write. If I hadn't, it would have been absurd for me to stand up in front of a writing class to preach the virtues of free expression in a democracy, to teach the virtues of essays such as "Politics and the English Language," and then step out of the classroom too frightened about losing my job to say what I thought.

I wrote and wrote at OSU for the sheer love of writing. I published stories, articles, essays, reviews, profiles, interviews, and a novel. Then I wrote about Oregon State for the first time after a tenured colleague threatened to report me in the English chair, Bob Frank, because I asked why composition scholars wrote so many textbooks and ignored the working conditions of writing instructors. I wrote "Educating Joshua," a loud little essay printed as commentary by a Eugene weekly on November 16, 1989. I told the governor of Oregon what it had been like for me to teach his son, Joshua, in the English Department that lost Bernard Malamud.

Two-time Pulitzer Prize-winner and then chair of the OSU Journalism Department, Jon Franklin, told me that "Joshua" was "a nice piece of writing." Another OSU journalism professor wrote a note to tell me that "Joshua" was "uniformly excellent." A retired Portland professor wrote, "Bravo! You exposed some aspects of 'higher education' of which most taxpayers are ignorant. It was a difficult thing to do and I deeply admire and respect your efforts." A woman who refused to give me her name phoned to tell me Malamud had been given a "dry promotion" (new title, no raise) at OSU after he'd won his first National.

But when Bob Frank called me to his office on November 29, 1989, I had a feeling we weren't meeting to discuss accolades given the glares I'd gotten from several English faculty during the previous two weeks. The assistant chair sat in on the meeting as a witness while his boss yelled at me, called me sundry names, and said he should have gotten rid of me at the end of my first year. He also claimed that I'd made a public statement of my intent to leave OSU in a "recent article" and wanted to know if he could "count on me" for the next term.

The intent he alluded to was in the last paragraph, which read: "I'm leaving OSU the first chance I get. I'm fed up with cheating students out of their hard-earned literacy dollars." But Frank knew that in 1988, the Liberal Arts dean told instructors to look for work because most would not be chosen to stay on by the tenure system created for instructors for the first time in OSU history. It was created shortly after the AFT effort was stopped and just as OSU was hiring the even cheaper labor of graduate students entering the new College of Liberal Arts masters program. Frank knew, then, that I was seeking work and knew he'd written a letter of recommendation for me in July of 1988. And more than one instructor had either left or had been terminated during the middle of an academic year without any concern expressed by Frank. So it was obvious to me within two minutes after the November 29 meeting began, that Frank was making an attempt to force me out of my job for writing something the OSU power elite did not like. I asked him bluntly at that point, "Is this a setup?"

Frank didn't admit it, of course, but I needed no direct admission from him that I was being punished for something I wrote. I found abundant evidence elsewhere that the Oregon State University leadership wanted to silence me as much as the reactionary chair of the Cascadia College English Department in *A New Life* wanted to silence a pain in his ass by the name of Sy Levin. The two week delay between publication of "Joshua" and the November 29 meeting had nothing to do with the time it took OSU administrators to read the essay. It took that long for the OSU legal staff to devise a plan for forcing me off campus without appearing to violate my First Amendment rights.

Two days after the meeting, an ACLU representative I talked with confirmed that the meeting had been structured to avoid a technical First Amendment violation. "Joshua" was never mentioned by name during the meeting, nor shown to me, though Frank paraphrased the last paragraph when he glanced at the corner of a sheet of paper buried under other papers on his desk. Nor did he give me written notice that I was being fired. But if he had gotten me to agree with him in front of a witness that I'd made a public announcement of my intent to leave OSU, then he could have claimed I'd resigned, he could have claimed he'd done nothing to pressure me into resigning, and he could have claimed my leaving had nothing to do with his opinion of "Joshua," because he'd expressed no opinion in the meeting.

But the English Department chair taking any action was *prima facie* evidence of an attempt to punish me for writing "Educating Joshua." To begin with, I hadn't revealed any information not already public knowledge. In October of 1988, the state's largest newspaper, the Portland *Oregonian,* had printed a scathing critique by Western Oregon State College (untenured) English professor M. Elizabeth Wallace of the entire Oregon higher education system's treatment of writing instructors. Wallace was not fired. Frank could have ignored my essay as Wallace's essay was ignored. Second, Frank simply could have waited until I did leave the first chance I got, just as Malamud had done. Third, he could have refused to renew my contract after June of 1990 without cause, which he had the authority to do. Fourth, he could have waited until my scheduled tenure denial during the 1990-1991 academic year. Instead he attempted to intimidate me into resigning thirteen days after "Joshua" was published.

I found out what his incentive was few a hours after the November 29 meeting when a literature professor (who asked that I not use his name in any publication) came to my office to tell me he learned that the OSU president had read "Joshua" the day after it was published and had told the provost, Graham Spanier, to do something about it. Spanier called Frank and, according to the literature professor, "reamed" him out over the phone for thirty minutes. I gave Spanier four opportunities in writing to confirm or deny the phone call took place, but he would do neither.

I did get confirmation, however, on December 8, 1989, of how pervasive fear of speaking out was at Oregon State University. On December 8, the same literature professor who told me about the provost's phone call returned to tell me that many English Department faculty liked "Joshua" but were afraid to say anything to me about it, though one of that silent group did send a note (and asked me not to use his name in any publication), which read, "I was most distressed to hear you got canned. I thought 'Josh' was right on the money."

Being right on the money, though, wouldn't protect my job. Nor could I count on help from frightened colleagues worried about their own jobs. And a legal war would drive me into bankruptcy, win or lose. Still, like Malamud's Levin, I could not live with myself if I had to live with the obscenity of censorship. I fought back by continuing to write. On February 22, 1990, the Eugene weekly published "Paper Graders," a feature article I wrote to expose abusive working conditions for all instructors at the University of Oregon, and, at the same time, to refute the usual response to open dissent. "Paper Graders" corroborated the Wallace article and made it difficult to say that

"Joshua" was an isolated complaint written by one disgruntled instructor. "Academic Freedom?", a sidebar written by the managing editor, told readers about the attempt to force me out of my job for First Amendment use.

The response to "Paper Graders" was as strong as it was for "Joshua." A retired UO professor wrote to the weekly that "Barry Greer's article 'Paper Graders' is superb! It is the absolute truth not only about the University of Oregon, but about American universities in general." A UO instructor forced out of his job wrote, "I would like to praise the article 'Paper Graders' for exposing the conspiracy that has been taking place . . . at the UO."

But a reaction heard statewide came on Friday, March 8, 1990, when the Corvallis, Oregon daily paper ran a front-page story with this headline: "Governor rips 'paranoid' faculty." The article lead read: "A combative Gov. Neil Goldschmidt butted heads with the Oregon State University Faculty Senate on Thursday, saying faculty members tend to be 'paranoid' and unwilling to accept responsibility for 'junk' work being produced on campus." The Salem and Portland papers also carried the story.

I wasn't called down to Frank's office after "Paper Graders" was printed, and OSU renewed my contract for the next academic year. My chair apparently had forgotten he couldn't count on me--to legitimize censorship, OSU would have to use the bogus tenure system.

One anecdote is all that's needed to give you an idea of how asinine (to put it kindly) that tenure decision was. Three of the people who conspired in the attempt to force my resignation in 1989 had power a year later in my tenure decision: the assistant chair, the chair, and the provost. I asked each to not participate because of conflict of interest. The assistant chair ignored the request, Frank wrote me a note to say that "Educating Joshua" would not affect his decision, but Graham Spanier was the most ludicrous of the three when he tried to appear to have withdrawn from participation before I asked him to do so.

On February 26, 1991, Spanier wrote to me to say, "I have no intention of participating in your promotion and tenure review. On December 6, 1990, I notified Associate Vice President John Dunn that I was disqualifying myself on the grounds that there may be a perception of a conflict of interest (see enclosed memo)." The conflict, Spanier later said, was due to mention of his spouse in "Educating Joshua" and had nothing to do with any phone call he may have made to the English chair. But the provost had painted himself into a corner. His February 26th letter was dated six days after the College of Liberal Arts dean wrote that "you [Barry Greer] will not be reappointed to the faculty of the Department of English after expiration of your current contract on June 15, 1991." The dean wrote his official tenure denial letter on February 20 and hand delivered it to me in a meeting at his office on February 22. I recorded the meeting after getting his permission to do so, and when I asked him if my dossier would go on to the committee the provost sat on, the dean said, "This one will not go to central administration. The decision has been made here. It stops here."

Spanier never had reason to withdraw from participation and sent me a copy of his December 6 withdrawal memo *not* in December but only after I asked him, in writing, to withdraw on February 20, 1991. I have every reason to believe, then, that the

December 6 memo was a fabrication.

*

Given my experience at OSU, I think it's fair to conclude that the fiction of Malamud's *A New Life* was and still is not so far removed from the facts of academic reality at Oregon State. The McCarthy-era censorship Malamud described and the Reagan-era censorship I experienced both prevented even a semblance of intellectual freedom at OSU.

I also think it's fair to conclude that one major reason for lack of freedom in the OSU English Department was that reading literature had become the study of literature. English Department faculty could disconnect their own lives from the value of free expression inherent in the prose and poetry they read, studied, wrote, and lectured about. Literature had been reduced to an object of analysis, a philosophical riddle to be solved, a vehicle for promotion and tenure, or an assignment due Monday. Literature and life were no longer connected. *A New Life* therefore was ignored as an indictment of intellectual and moral corruption at OSU. The novel was dismissed by the babble of symposia as little more than another post-war existential schlemiel story.

With wonderful Malamudian irony, though, my experience at OSU reconnected my life to art and brought me back to questions more personal and powerful than any symposia paper would dare ask. From November of 1989 when "Joshua" was published until June of 1991 when I was forced out of my job, I came back again and again to two questions I imagine Levin would have asked himself had he lived on as a character after *A New Life* ended. One. Was it worth the price I paid? No. I have no doubt whatsoever that a writer teaching in a public university English department financed by an elected legislature should not have paid the price I paid for using the First Amendment. My loss was over a half million dollars: the sum of lost income, the price of paying my own health insurance, and the value my pension would have had at retirement if I hadn't used it to supplement unemployment benefits.

Two. And most important. Knowing when I wrote "Educating Joshua" that my words would do nothing to end corruption, should I have written the essay? Yes. Even after Malamud-the-dead-writer was interred and memorialized and safely in the hands of the scholars, OSU remained embarrassed by him and tucked his memory into a small upstairs sitting room. The university wanted the reflected glory of Malamud-the-cultural-monument and wanted to exorcise the ghost of Malamud-the-pain-in-the-ass. It failed to do so. Malamud-the-monument would forever be on the literary map while OSU remained a blank spot. In his *New York Times Book Review* front-page Malamud obituary, Philip Roth could not remember where in Oregon Malamud had taught, though he remembered what Malamud wrote. "Bern taught nearby at the state university in Eugene (pop. 50,000) since leaving New York (pop. 8,000,000) and a night school teaching job there in 1949--12 years in the Far West instructing freshman Oregonians the fundamentals of English composition and writing his unorthodox baseball novel, 'The Natural,' his masterpiece set in darkest Brooklyn, 'The Assistant,' as well as four or five of the best American short stories I'd ever read (or ever will)." Malamud kept the integrity of his talent and his intellect in darkest Oregon. Malamud had not been silenced by the small minds he found in the Oregon State College English Department. Both his life and his art were devoted to freedom of expression. Near the end of *A New Life* Gerald Gilley, sterile cuckold, confronted Sy Levin, fertile Jew and fired writing instructor from New York City who refused to be silenced. "Why take that load on yourself?" Gilley wanted to know, referring to the price Levin paid for love and First Amendment use. "Because," said Levin, "I can, you son of a bitch." How could I have taught and wrote where Malamud taught and wrote and have remained silent? Yes, I'd do it again. I'd write a loud little essay about teaching writing to the son of Oregon's Jewish governor at the university where Malamud the Jew taught, in the town where Malamud the Jew wrote about suffering and love and redemption.

And freedom.

Short version originally printed on front page of
Writer's N.W. *in March of 1993.*

THE GRADES OF WRATH

Richard Hill

Me and Estrellita come up from Homestead with Joaquin, Dierdre, Gesner the little Haitian, and the Obligado brothers to work the fall harvest. We didn't even bother to look for housing but slept in the bus at the edge of campus and went to the English Department to apply and waited to see if enrollment would be anything like the bumper crop we'd heard about. Dierdre grumbled the whole time. She wanted to go back and pick lettuce, then beans, then navel oranges and tangerines. It was real hot, and we had to walk a long way to find some dorm showers we could use.

"Why you want to pick?" I asked Dierdre. "This is white-collar work. This is America." She just fan herself with one of the textbooks and look out the bus window with that black face of hers like a mean squall coming off the Gulf. "Jamaicans too proud to do this work," she said. "This is stoop labor. I rather cut cane." She helped Estrellita cook, but she wouldn't sing with us after dinner.

It was a bumper crop, the highest freshman enrollment ever. We all got four sections Freshman Comp except little Gesner, who got two comps and two

ESLs, which was by then about the only thing could make Dierdre smile. She said English was his second language, all right--a long second. Even we had trouble understanding little Gesner, but he was a cheerful little dude and did his class preparations just like he could read. We had it worked out that we all got our MFAs in different places and Gesner was Cajun, but they didn't ask us for no papers.

Dierdre got sick before midterms. First it was just throwing up and headaches, then she just stopped meeting her students and laid around all the time in the bus and wouldn't eat nothing but Burger King milk shakes. We didn't have no student benefits because we was faculty and no faculty benefits because we was temporary. The local welfare couldn't help because we wasn't U.S. citizens, though that never kept them from deducting our taxes. The campus doctor did look once at her before he found out she wasn't no student from Zaire and said it looked like depression to him. He wrote a prescription for pills that we couldn't afford. Dierdre stayed on her cot with the Burger King milk shakes and a copy of Huckleberry Finn. At least the weather cooled off.

She was a little better by Thanksgiving and went with us to the cafeteria for dinner, but the next time I saw her she was packed and heading for the Greyhound station. "I'm goin' south," she said. "Don't try to stop me!"

I didn't. We all talked about it that night. How could she give up being a teacher in an American university? "Ai, chihuahua, but she's proud," Estrellita said. "Too proud for her own good." We decided to send her some money as soon as we could. We got a few postcards from her over the spring semester. We were all busting our tails to keep up and never got enough money ahead to send her any. She said she'd worked the lettuce again, the snap beans, the Valencias and grapefruit. She said she could breathe deep again and didn't even mind the pesticides, snakes and skeeters.

One thing about teaching, the time passes quick. Before we knew it our final grades were due. Little Gesner got hired for the summer, but the rest of us got cut loose. We'd been hearing rumors about a budget crunch here and a big crop of freshmen due next year in North Carolina. We headed up there in late August, but the rumors was false and only Estrellita and one of the Obligados got hired, part time. It was tough. Me and Joaquin and the other Obligado scratched for work, but we didn't find much. We wouldn't have made it through that winter if it wasn't for the money Dierdre sent.

First published by In These Times, *Sept. 19-25, 1990*

COME WALK WITH ME

Mark Hillringhouse

(after Po' Chu-i)

Don't go off and become a teacher,
you'll only make yourself miserable.
Come June you'll realize you'll be working all summer
just to make ends meet.
When it's time for bed you'll be up grading papers.
The IRS will hit you over and over again for new taxes
and you'll never be able to save more than a week's pay.
Come walk with me and together
we will launch a boat and watch the ripples
our oars make in the water as we drift
far, very far, away from shore.

EVENING IN PATERSON

Mark Hillringhouse

(after Lu Yu)

Here in the damaged city
evening falls peacefully.
Half woosy, I sprawl in the hallway.
A streetlamp shines in the polluted
sky. The wind is so gentle the leaves
are hardly ruffled. I have escaped
from lies and trouble. I no longer
work at the college. I no longer
have any importance. I do not
miss my office or my boring
meetings. Here at home
I have plenty to be afraid of.

THE OTHER DAY

Charles Hood

it happened again
(it's not my fault!),
another disaster,
another movie scene
following me around
like a three-legged mongrel.
This time it was at the staff meeting,
the light from the west painting the room
a greasy shade of yellow, when
I heard the hoof beats coming,
saying to myself, *man,
not again,* not at four in the afternoon
after three comp sections,
but it was too late to stop it
and this time they were Saracens
or maybe Turks, they came too fast
to tell, one riding a huge sorrel
right through the window,
glass everywhere, his sword
bright as chrome, two more
pantalooned berserkers
coming through the door,
as my briefcase spilled open
dumping a Webley pistol into my lap
and I stood on the table
elbows locked, feet in a line
with my hips, the shots

crashing out like car accidents
happening over and over.
I had to reload twice and there was
even a bit of hand-to-hand
fighting towards the end.
It was hell trying to keep it
out of the papers and none
of us could hear right for days
(never shoot a gun indoors),
but to be honest with you
the window was dirty and
had not opened right for years,
and the department chair's funeral
will be next Tuesday, all classes
canceled, even though Eva, she's
the secretary, she really does
all the work and everybody knows it,
and none of the rest of us really
could stand him anyway.

First published in 1994 by inside english.

WHEN HE WAS PATIENT

Maria Theresa Maggi

When he was patient, which was hardly ever,
he cut words like a jeweler would facet a stone,
wasting no stroke that would grab and hold light.
But mostly, he slacked off on his papers
just enough, in just such a way
that anyone who really wanted to find out
what was going on would have to ask him in person.
She was grateful she had always written comments in pencil.
Inevitably, whatever she wrote she'd give up
and scrawl *see me in office hours,*
then wait, hope she'd know what to say.
He'd come on Thursday afternoons,
wait until everyone else was done talking.
Then he'd saunter in and sit down, grinning.
He liked this part especially.
But he couldn't talk too long
about his own writing.   He'd get edgy,
look away, though he'd never leave because of it.
Okay. They talked about music, the full moon,
what kind of food they liked,
car accidents they'd been in, what made them laugh.
The janitor got used to cleaning up around them.

He told her why he joined a fraternity,
why he came to Idaho, whether or not he thought
about what happens after we die.
He said he thought about it all the time.
He had a friend who accidentally killed a girl.
She had fallen into the water last summer.
The lake was black and sharp, curling up
and twisting back over itself, folding her
like a piece of scrap paper,
and he could not turn the propeller
on his boat off in time.
He thought this friend took it too hard,
blamed it on himself for too long.
Alone, she'd think about that boy, working
in another university cafeteria across the country,
throwing dirty plates into a huge gray plastic tub
gaping open like a cheap coffin that can never be sealed.
We can't judge what constitutes suffering
for other people, she said, when he was callously
judgmental of something else they had read in class.
He just looked at her, mildly annoyed, and said *I guess not.*

I ENDED UP LIKING HER

Maria Theresa Maggi

I ended up liking her in spite of myself,
because she kept on surprising me.
One afternoon I was up in the English Department
trying to get out again, to explain what I had already done
to satisfy this stupid writing requirement.
I wasn't supposed to be in this cheesy class.
I paid $60.00 to take an advanced placement exam
and I scored high enough to exempt out.
The university wanted additional verification,
they wanted their own tag on it,
they wanted to babysit me. I was pissed.
The secretary was giving me her stone face.
Then in she comes to look at her mail or something.
She stops in the middle of the floor
to put her finger over her left ear.
Then she opened her mouth.
"My ears are plugged," she said,
and laughed. Then she looked right at me
and said, "What are you doing here,
trying to drop my class?"
All I could do was smile like an idiot.
How did she know and not know at the same time?

One day I even turned on the lights for her
in front of everybody. They were all so dull
with the exception of two or three others that
we could have been having the class alone.
Sometimes it was as if we were alone
in the middle of all those people.
Still, having that audience was a blast.
I even saw how I could like writing,
it wasn't so bad. I won her silly
Paper Clip Award for Best Peer Editor.
All that process and meta-process stuff
she learned in California wasn't too bad, either.
I liked pleasing her more than I felt comfortable with.
And she thought I had no choice.
She didn't have any idea I could take that test
and just split in the middle of the semester.
I couldn't tell her it would all be over soon.
She sweats everything too much.

GOD'S TRUTH

Christina McVay

I am descended from the Puritans on my father's side, and, as I was growing up, my father in many ways personified some of those old Calvinist virtues: you get up early, you work hard, you don't waste time, you live modestly, you keep your promises, and you pay your debts. Not all of those virtues took hold: I love to sleep in, and sometimes I find myself wasting time without feeling particularly guilty. But I do live modestly (and like to think I would continue to do so even if I won the lottery); I try to keep promises; and I have always been conscientious about paying bills.

Though a single mother in graduate school, I managed to maintain a good credit rating. Consequently, I kept getting credit cards in the mail. Lots of them. And, yes, I did use them, but *not* frivolously. To anyone who knows me, it is very obvious that I haven't bought myself new clothes in a long time. This is the first winter in five years that I've had a pair of boots, and they were a gift. (On an anonymous evaluation of my teaching, a student once commented that it was difficult to take seriously a person who wore the same shabby clothes every day.) But the car needs brakes? I didn't figure that into my budget. Get out the Firestone Card. I have to get a prescription filled? MasterCard time. The boys need shoes for foothall? Sears. The only luxury I allowed myself to be talked into was a stereo from Penney's. Now, I have not considered myself a religious person for a long time, but I have to admit, when six months after that purchase my house was burglarized and the stereo stolen, the thought crossed my mind that maybe God was punishing me for that extravagance. In truth, though, while I was accumulating debts, I assumed I would one day have a real job and be able to pay them off.

How naive.

Two and a half years ago, right about the time I was beginning work on my dissertation in earnest, I had no choice but to join the ranks of Kent State's part-time instructors, which meant I also had to start paying back student loans.

This made it difficult to make even the minimum payments on my other debts. Reluctantly, but in an honest effort to pay my bills, I started working part-time evenings and weekends at the new supermarket down the street. I thought I could get my head above water in six months, maybe a year. I'm still weighing produce and bulk foods. My dissertation is dead.

A year ago, my brother, who has a history of heart problems, became sick again, had to quit his job, and moved in with me. It was six months before he finally started receiving disability, so I was feeding and housing him, and paying for his medication. That put me over the edge. I had to start thinking seriously about bankruptcy.

It was a hard decision. Where I come from, it's copping out. My ancestors haunted me: "These are honest debts, and you have to pay them honestly. You knew that when you used those cards. It doesn't matter that Visa has made a profit off you with their outrageous finance charges. You knew that was how the game is played." I put off as long as I could talking to a lawyer. I had to do it, but I was not comfortable with it. My father's reaction surprised me: "Well, these days it's not that big a deal." (I can't help but wonder whether his recent conversion to Catholicism doesn't have something to do with this new attitude.) I, however, was still not happy.

Today, I drove to the Federal Building in Akron for my final hearing. I felt sick, literally. I sat next to my lawyer in the Bankruptcy Courtroom *sweating* while Federal Bankruptcy Judge H. F. White called people up in front of him, asked a few questions, and usually granted their cases. It was simple. Two minutes and you're done. God was punishing me again, though--I was almost the last person on the judge's list.

At last, my turn came. My lawyer said his lawyerly stuff, and Judge White, a soft-spoken, elderly and efficient man, asked me where I worked.

"I teach part-time at Kent State University, and I also work part-time in a grocery store." I wanted him to know I really had tried.

"What do you teach?"

"Well, I teach part-time in the English Department and part-time in the German Department."

He looked up from the papers in his hands and asked, "Don't you know you can earn more at MacDonald's?"

Imagine my bewilderment. "What?!"

"I hope Kent State pays their part-timers better than the University of Akron does."

"No, your Honor, I think it's about the same." "Well, then, you *could* do better at MacDonald's." As what he was saying sank in, I couldn't help it—I laughed and said nervously, "I am *amazed* that you're aware of this situation."

"Aware! Of course I'm aware of the situation, he said in a rather loud voice. "I teach part-time in Akron's School of Law."

This little conversation was so unexpected that I just blurted out, "Oh, my God, then we're colleagues."

"Yes, indeed. . . ." He continued talking for another minute or so, but my mind was too confused to follow what he said. I do recall words like "disgraceful" and "scandalous." The next thing I knew, my case was granted, and the next person's name was called.

I left the courtroom and smiled all the way down the elevator and out to my car. I turned the radio up and enjoyed a wonderful drive home. This man, after all, this *judge* had understood, and forgiven me. The guilt was gone. It was as good as going to church is supposed to be. And it's true. It's in the Federal Court records.

DE+SIDUS

Naomi Rachel

*A Ph.D. in sixteenth century literature. Four volumes of
poetry. Well reviewed. Major reputation plus years of
teaching at university level. Intense desire to teach
freshman comp. Eleven thousand five hundred. Normal
load: four courses per quarter.*

Desire. De+sidus. From stars. To await from stars.
It's that bright one that could pass for a planet.
Left of the milky way. Living there is the one
all job lists are written to. Mr. Star.
A poet of heavenly verse. With all the trappings.
And he loves, ah how he loves freshman comp.
Each and every part of speech. Each under-prepared
student is indeed exceptional to him.
Yes he's the one who fills all those jobs.
Short. Neat. Affable but stern.
Portly but never offensive.
Diagramming sentences brightened by starlight,
his bald head shines a beam of knowledge.

OPEN SEASON IN CHICAGO

A.L. Reilly

The last class I taught at Karegian College had a Wonderland quality. It was diverse; it was unruly; it was charmingly unpredictable. But unlike Alice, I came to the realization that I had fallen down the wrong rabbit hole. In Alice's hole, at least there was someone to tell her what to do, "Eat me" or "Drink me" or "Hush!" At Karegian College, a four-year institution deep in the center of the American heartland, there were no such services.

Of course in my three years there, I'd already learned that. On the first day of my first semester, a student had had a heart attack. I raced him to the office.

"Do we have an infirmary?" I asked the work-aid student, who was eating potato chips and staring vacantly at a poster announcing a poetry reading by Maya Angelou two years before.

"No," she said.

"Well--what do I do?"

"I dunno," she shrugged, swallowing a potato chip.

"Can I use the phone?"

"I dunno."

The third day of my second semester, a student tried to commit suicide by ingesting 60 Midol; she sat in the back of the classroom as I extolled the virtues of the topic sentence, which, while extensive, do not often inspire seizures. I caught her--literally--as she slid down the yellow wall. She lived, only to fall into crisis three weeks later. That second time, we had to discuss her problems in the bathroom. (Part-timers had no offices.)

"My mother was nutso," began one essay by a student who later wrote her persuasion paper supporting the continued sale of Prozac. She had found her mother dead on the floor of the living room.

Clearly, this was a population with needs. But when I'd mentioned the "nutso" essay at one of our few part-time faculty meetings (the paper wasn't well-written, I'd explained--but how do I grade a thing like that?) "Oh, I've gotten papers like that," veterans replied. "Just grade it."

Slowly it became clear that K.C.'s open admission policy meant open season. K.C.'s student body consisted of children who had survived the open season that had been declared on them in 1980. Now it was their turn. Now it was open season on any adult who inadvertently--through syllabi, reading lists, or rules--blocked the inevitable advance of entropy. It was Wonderland with a domino theory.

And it was politically correct--no tracking, no threshold testing: a texthook of essays devoted just to diversity; and a process-oriented teaching style that eschewed any reference to imperialist concepts like sentences, periods, or commas for the first two semesters of writing. Students roamed in and out of class like kids at a matinee, and it was not unusual to see a student once a month.

Gregory, hostile, outspoken, non-linear, had come once a month. He'd submitted two prose poems addressed to a woman he loved. As far as I understood them, he felt a violent, agonizing need to be with her; he resented her cagey evasions and coquettish come-ons; and he himself was teetering on the bloodied knife-edge of psychic pain and suicide. Taking my "nutso" experience in hand, I addressed form, format, and style. "It's not an essay," I told him. "It's interesting, but it doesn't have a thesis that is supported by clearly delineated evidence."

I was proven wrong--thesis and evidence were very clear. After meeting with me, Gregory had dropped the poems off at the woman's house. She'd called the police, who, after they read them, arrested him for stalking. He later told me that the police thought he was self-destructive and had put him in a padded cell. "Ignorant bastards," he scoffed, showing me his electronic homing device, which put him under "house arrest." "Fancy that," I said, recalling a poetic image depicting the slow, joyous torture of Eden's snake.

We were never, never to deny students access-- although we had no way to help students who needed more than a couple of lessons on paragraphs. People who needed lessons on how to read or how to treat their fellow human beings were flat out of luck. All they had was us--a motley group of M.A.s without backup--and this hold on us was absolute.

It was that sense of being held hostage that made me rebel. The next semester I threw a 240-pound drunk student out of class for referring to me as a "fucking teacher bitch" on his diagnostic. For two weeks I worried about being fired.

But that was before the last semester. During the last semester, I wondered if there were any opportunities for getting fired that I'd perhaps overlooked.

The last group made "It's a Small World After All" look like an exclusive golf club. Of 22 students, one young man had AIDS, one woman was deaf, one woman had recently been beaten by her Lesbian lover, and one woman (unmarried) was well into her third trimester. We had five black students, 13 WASPs, one WASC, one Cambodian, one Jew, and one Hispanic. The deaf woman was white; her interpreter was black and confided that she found whites inexpressive and nearly unreadable. In one corner of the room was an art student, Aaron, who was unable to copy a sentence but was nonetheless the art department's star, renowned for his conceptual work. In the other corner was blue-eyed Peter, a serious suburbanite whose essay on homeless people argued that those of us with homes had good reasons for ignoring beggars in the streets.

Alice would have gone along for the ride and enjoyed herself. But I had resolved to teach. I taught subjects and verbs and Robert Staples' "Night Walker." I taught commas and quotes and Martin Luther King's "I Have a Dream." Then I gave a test, and then I started all over again. Papers came in three, four, eight weeks late. The interpreter came in 10, 20, 40 minutes late, plunging Tracy, the deaf student, into profound disconnect. Students disappeared, reappeared, demanded reparations. The Cambodian student, writing in a second language, got the highest score on a test on punctuation. This was crazier than Wonderland. This was Oz in a funhouse mirror.

In a brand new part-time faculty office, a closet with three desks in it, the stories of burnout started rolling in. I empathized with a faculty member who worried that her students had organized a petition against her. "Don't worry," I heard someone tell her, "they won't be able to find the administration either."

Perhaps understanding the administrative structure at K.C., the artist's mother began to call me. "What did Aaron get on the test?" she asked.

"A 14 out of a 100," I answered.

"You're not going to flunk him, are you? He needs this class to graduate."

Somewhere near the ninth week, a dean came to see me. I knew there were deans, but I'd seen one in the flesh only once before and had since come to believe that he was a hologram. This time he explained that Sabrina, whom I hadn't seen in four weeks, was pregnant and due two weeks after graduation.

"Graduation?" I asked. "She doesn't need this class to graduate, does she?"

"She's a good student," he said.

"She can't identify a sentence," I said.

"She's a good student," he said.

"What am I supposed to do?"

"She's a good student," he said.

So I began to tutor Sabrina on my own time (which I believe brought my wages down to about 75 cents an hour). The dean immediately beamed up to his mothership and cut all communications.

Aaron's mother was another story.

"You're not going to flunk him, are you?" Mrs. S. asked. "I'm widowed and he needs this grade to graduate, and they don't offer this during the summer."

"Sure they do."

"He's already taking history this summer. I'm widowed and disabled and what are we going to do?"

"I can't help you," I heard myself say, cringing at this scandalous truth. In our last conversation, she offered me a bribe.

By that time I realized that this was Oz without a wicked witch; and it was Oz before the Wizard was reactivated. That's a dangerous kind of Oz to have: There was no single enemy, and there was no man behind the curtain. The causes of our problems were as diverse as the students, 18 of whom had never heard of the Civil War, and I was just a little munchkin, an M.A. without a broomstick.

Still, we ended up a little more cohesive than we began. In a final grammar game, Aaron snuck up to the board to change the scores and was caught by Tracy, who signed so indignantly that her interpreter started shouting. As the game ended, those who had won fabulous prizes cheered, checked their Lotto tickets and flaunted their Wonder Bubbles. But it was not a clean sweep: The vociferous Sheila demanded an incomplete and my chair agreed (bringing my salary down to just 50 cents an hour) and, after Mrs. S.'s attempted bribe, someone in the elusive counseling office admitted that Aaron didn't need my course to graduate after all.

"Does Aaron know this?" I asked.

"I told him two months ago," said the counselor.

In the end, some of the writing was extraordinary. But there was always a sense that we were just making due, that we were all survivors of open season. Castaways in a cultural war. This saddened me. For if I felt like a lonely breakwater beating back a tide of wild waves threatening the last vestiges of intellectual order, they must have felt a little uncertain riding those cresting giants.

Oh, for a few lifeboats!

TO KEEP SEARCHING
FOR THE STOLEN CHILD

Mary Rohrer-Dann

In Fiction Writing class, give your students suggestions for a ten-minute freewrite: something that makes them furious; their first sexual experience; I am Joe's kidney; I am Jo's uterus. After intense scribbling by both you and your students, ask for volunteers to read their freewrites aloud. Sometimes you read your own, but not today. You've written an extravagant invective to the rejection that came this morning for the book you've been trying to get published the last eighteen months. The paper's blistering. Randy, a sweet boy with pale auburn hair and startling golden eyes, raises his hand. In an earnest voice, he reads about his first blowjob--a 17th birthday present from his girlfriend. It happened in his father's cramped Toyota on a sticky July night in the King of Prussia Mall parking lot. With Madonna proclaiming on the radio, Randy's girlfriend went to town, muffling his pleasured moans with a sock and mumbling something about satisfying her 2000 daily caloric requirement. Never look at this student again without seeing him with his pants down around his knees and a sock stuffed in his mouth.

Talk daily about showing not telling, about multi-faceted characters, vigorous verbs. Illustrate with examples from Welty, Coover, Dubus, Hempel. Deliver witty sermons about flabby language, the sins of adjectives and adverbs, passive voice. Sense yourself becoming in their eyes not unlike those high school English teachers with damp fingers and a fondness for unusual plaids who told you never to begin a sentence with "but."

In your first batch of student stories are two about amnesia victims, three about witty, urbane homeless people, two hijackings, several murders, a murderous ghost, a grandmother who you'd like to murder, and more than a few stories about trying to write a story for this class. Now you know how influential Movie of the Week and Afternoon Special are, how common feces fixations, and just how deep misogyny runs. When asked about their favorite authors your students confirm your suspicions: Stephen King is king and Harlequin is queen.

At home, sneak off to the bathroom several times a day where you keep a decadently rich anthology of international short fiction on the tank top of your toilet. Lock yourself in and read whole stories at a sitting, gorging like a bulemic.

In the new coffee shop downtown, sip Raspberry Truffle, creamy with half and half, and butter muffin after blueberry muffin as you read and grade papers. It seems as if you are always reading other people's writing, which wouldn't be so bad perhaps if the writing you were reading was any good. In student stories, eyes have a tendency to fall to the floor (do they roll, you wonder, under the fridge?); profusely sweating fugitives create small waves in the ponds they gaze into; stewardesses flash airbrushed gums while airline passengers throw up into overhead compartments; and lovers cling together like leftovers in Saran Wrap.

Admit you're not being fair. Some of the stories are good. One or two are very good; good enough to make the green snake raise its tapered head--you were thirty before you could write the way this kid writes at nineteen. Whisper platitudes to yourself about late bloomers. Tillie Olsen was 48 when *Tell Me A Riddle* was published; Grace Paley, 37, when *The Ten Little Disturbances of Man* came out. Better to reach your peak at 80 than 40, except that no one in your family has made it past 75. You have no pretensions of genius, but wonder if you're as mediocre as you're beginning to feel. Think of William Kennedy. *Ironweed* took ten years to publish. Then remember John Kennedy Toole. After a decade of rejection, he shot himself in the head. Determined to get justice, his mother took the manuscript to Walker Percy, gave him no peace until he read it. He did, made sure it got published. National Book Award.

You don't need a Pushcart or a Pen/Faulkner award, you just want your damn book published. Of course, your standing in the department might rise considerably if you were dead. Maybe you could be awarded tenure posthumously. It worked for Toole.

But no one in your family reads.

Finish five more student papers and reward yourself with yet another muffin. Apple cinnamon this time. Consider taking up smoking to reduce the eating frenzy grading induces. You've gained an average of three pounds per semester since you started teaching six years ago; at this rate, you're destined for sumo thighs and a gut to match. Three more papers, then take a break.

Move to the other coffee shop around the block: their soggy pastries tempt less.

Outside, the air is like ground glass. But the orgy of colored leaves doesn't fool you--there's annihilation in that blue sky. Fall always depresses you. Another year and you're no closer to publication. The agent you've been trying to hook up with doesn't return your calls; editors rave about how powerful you writing is, how it's gutsy and takes risks but it's not what we're looking for right now though we wish you luck in placing it elsewhere. Think about starting your own small press. Call it *Elsewhere.* Without that book you're no closer to a secure job or even one that commands respect or simply a decent wage. Your biological clock is processing time in nano-seconds and yon're deathly afraid people can spot you instantly for an English teacher.

A little whirlwind of cold air sends dead leaves skittering across your shoes. When you enter the coffee shop, the dark, oily odor of expresso slides around you like a premonition. Maybe it's just those tech writing papers waiting in your bookbag that fills you with dread. Fifty of them. But look on the bright side: grounded in research, in other people's work, the tech papers offer a respite from the weird and often puny undergraduate imagination. And, hey, you've picked up all kinds of fascinating factoids, great for conference dinners and faculty parties.

For example, how best to execute death-row prisoners. From a ten-page evaluation paper, you learn that electrocution sizzles the body like a french fry. The internal organs cook and the skin sears and splits, requiring a three-minute cool-down before the body can be touched.   Cost-effectiveness rules out the gas chamber, and hanging often results in the prisoner gagging to death--too cruel and unusual. Lethal injection wins hands down.   The author, an Administration of Justice major in his late twenties, a MENSA member who's worked as a prison guard and plans to be a warden, looks at you with eyes black and bullet-hard, as if deciding what crimes you might be capable of.

In private conference with him you tend to stutter.

Another tech writing student regularly details, in the anonymous student evaluations you periodically request, everything he hates: you, this class, the stupid people in it, the stupid assignments, the stupid computer lab assistants who deliberately screw him over. Most of all he hates "that feminist crap"--the readings you assign for discussion and rhetorical analysis. "Why do we need to read this shit?" he writes. Why, indeed. You know who he is because he always writes in red ink. He is a pre-med student, the one who wants to be a gynecologist.

Grade three more papers, then get another cup of coffee, decaf this time--the words are shimmying on the page.   See your old student Carlos float by the front window in hand-tooled leather cowboy boots and jeans that look painted on, a huge silver belt hanging on those slender hips. His pale face is beautiful and vacant, his doe eyes unfocused, a tic winking in his unshaven cheek. Carlos has sold himself for dope and a place to sleep since he was seven; he's out to lunch for good.

The first week you had him in your freshman comp class, three years ago when you were new in town and all you could get was an adjunct position, you gave him your home phone and told him to call if he ran into trouble with his essay. Midnight on Friday the phone rings and there's Carlos, higher than the World Trade Center, asking in his caterpillar voice why you wanted him to call. He assumes you are a buyer or a trick.

You wonder yourself, sometimes.

You do most of your grading in coffee shops or quiet bars because the refrigerator at home never stops its siren song and your office-mate Gregory has all but taken up residence in the cubicle the department claims is an office. Gregory now calls himself Gregorio, and his upstate New York speech has slid, over the semester, deeper into accent. By summer, he'll have dispensed with English altogether. Often, while you're discussing character development with a fiction student, he erupts into arias from *Tasca* or *The Ring*, enough vibrato in his voice to split an atom. "If your character is weird, you must know why he's weird," you say as Gregory/ Gregorio sweeps into the cubicle, exploding the cramped space with his rich baritone. "Know your character's motivation," you continue, wondering what Gregorio's is. Students complain that he sings his lectures and writes comments in "some foreign language" on their papers. They drop his courses faster than they drop their pants on a Saturday night so he always has a third fewer papers to grade.

Maybe Gregorio isn't all that nuts. Certainly no more than your former office-mate, a demure, elfin young woman who spoke in a murmuring voice and who liked to send fresh roadkill, exquisitely gift-wrapped, to people who had offended her--ex-lovers, ex-roommates, colleagues who'd somehow stepped on her toes. You're still not sure what you did to deserve the possum remains that arrived UPS one Saturday afternoon, although you suspect it was your inability to appreciate the panel session she chaired at a regional MLA conference: "A Necessary Construction: Vaginal Pride in Feminist Speculative Fiction." She has since moved on to a tenure-track position in California.

Remind yourself how fortunate you are to have a full-time position with a renewable one-year contract and some health benefits--enough to cover a hangnail or hemorrhoids, though not both. So many others work from semester to semester with no benefits at all, or hold three part-time jobs so they don't have to live on Happy Hours hors d'oeuvres. The department administrators view you and your fellow "amateurs" as obstacles to the university's "commitment to undergraduate education," even though you shoulder most of the lower level course load. Your shared non-status should give you solidarity, but the unspoken fact that the less-numerous male instructors are paid more than the females keeps you circling each other like starved dogs eyeing a hunk of bad meat.

Things could be worse. You could still be in public relations, pushing bathroom fixtures, selling your soul along with the porcelain, fearful you will never write a line that has any intrinsic worth or will change someone's life or at least linger in their mind for a moment or two.

But was industry so bad?

The company sent you all over the country to scout photos of their products--bathtubs, shower surrounds, pedestal sinks, pedestal toilets, spas, whirlpools, bidets. You hobnobbed with professional photographers and designers; you had an expense account. You've wandered through more pink-marbled, cavernous bathrooms of the nouveau riche than Robin Leach. You've been in more public men's rooms than your lover, sidling out of the tiled elegance with the lens cap off your Nikon and the flash on, smiling sweetly at the disconcerted man going in.

At least there you didn't have sweet-faced born-agains spitting poison at gay classmates, and education majors complaining about having to use the library. You knew you weren't pushing some pressure-cooked student permanently over the edge with the C- you gave him for his final grade. You didn't have a student collapsing in tears after class because she is pregnant and she doesn't believe in abortion but she doesn't want to be a mother yet either. And you didn't wake up at three in the morning with the image floating before you of the wooden-faced girl with colorless hair who confessed that, twice, she has tried to commit suicide, and that your comments on her last story kept her from trying it again over the weekend.

So why are you here? What's the point of sitting, impotent, listening to a student who has missed class for the past two weeks explain that she's been trying to find where her husband has hidden her son. She and her husband are American Indian, but of different tribes, and she suspects her son is somewhere on the Onondaga reservation where her husband grew up. She whispers when she speaks but her brown eyes behind the glasses are fierce. She asks for an extension on a paper already two weeks late, and you nod, embarrassed at the meagerness of what you can do for her. Touch her arm and know immediately you've made a mistake--one touch and she will shatter. But she is stronger than you think. She looks at you, eyes wet but unflinching, her grim smile revealing crooked, discolored teeth. Last semester when she took this course with you, before dropping out midway, she missed a week of classes when her husband's fists bruised two of her ribs and shook loose the teeth in her upper jaw.

Her garbled papers, full of wild punctuation, sentences that end in mid-thought or veer abruptly off-course, are written in a longhand that coils across the paper like barbed wire. She has no typewriter, can't come to campus at night to use the computers because she squeezes her classes between two jobs, all the while searching the bureaucratic labyrinth of social workers, lawyers, and the Bureau of Indian Affairs for her boy. She may never put a decent paragraph together but she will also never stop searching for her stolen child.

The door to the coffee shop blows open and Gregorio sweeps in, arrogance sliding off his Bram Stoker cape like fog. He pauses by your table, picks up the top paper in the fiction pile with fingers perfectly manicured. "And how are the little cretins coming along?" he says. "Any Sappho's in this gaggle? Voltaire's?" He laughs operatically and you notice how closely spaced his eyes are despite the aquiline nose. Ah, Gregorio, you think, don't worry about tenure. You've got the right stuff. Gregorio holds up the student paper, peering at it, his pale tongue flicking across his lips. "My, my, my," he says, "this one stars

Mr. Spock. How quaint. "

You look at the paper in his hand, see the writing in all capital letters, the black-inked strokes stiff and deep, as if the author's cutting words into flesh. Dan. A punker in black shirt, black jeans, black shoes, black slouch hat atop dyed black hair. Every story he writes is about a boy plotting to kill his father. When you told him to try something different, something from his own life, he looked at you for a long time, then walked out the door. The next week, you asked him to read his rough draft to the class. He always declined when you asked him before, but that time you were determined. You teased, cajoled. He shook his head. C'mon, you said, and then he did.

He read how his mother had been in and out of hospitals ever since he could remember. When depression hit, she'd curl up in a corner of her bathroom weeping; in her manic states she played records of Leonard Nimoy reading his poems. Dan would come home from school to a house reverberating with the voice of Mr. Spock, his mother flitting about the living room, words darting from her mouth like crazed butterflies. She'd pull him upstairs into the little room where she wrote her poetry. She'd read him what she had written that day, twenty, sometimes thirty pages.

The evening his father told his mother he was leaving for another woman, Dan escaped with his little brother to the movies. The feature had just begun when he heard his name paged in the dark theatre and knew his mother was dead. Running out into the rainy night, all Dan could think about was the *Star Trek* episode where Spock, fighting a virus that destroys his Vulcan self-control, weeps violently because he never told his human mother that he loved her. Like Spock, Dan repeated his name over and over and over until he had mastered himself and his eyes were dry as desert air.

The class sat stunned. You managed to say thank you, Dan. Later, when you tried to apologize for bullying him, he said, "I needed to write it."

You take the paper from Gregorio's damp fingers, place it carefully back on the pile. This is why you are here. To bear witness to their integrity and grace, to hear their stories, to remember. Through them you learn to keep searching for the stolen child, to reclaim the lost mother, to keep writing.

KICK 'EM WHILE THEY'RE DOWN

Ben Satterfield

When I taught at the University of Texas in the 70s and 80s I managed for the most part to avoid direct kicks, but I was constantly aware of my status, which was close to *persona non grata*. Although not shunned like pariabs, the temporary faculty were distinctly second-class citizens, tolerated but not encouraged. Historically, the regents of this mammoth institution have governed by jackboot, and the air of authority was pervasive, like tear gas in a closed room. Brooking no complaints, the regents ruled from their tower like the gods of Olympus. A lawsuit once had to be filed by the Texas Faculty Association (a union-like organization) on behalf of the University of Texas faculty in order to secure policy changes in the Regents Rules & Regulations, a sad commentary on the attitudes of the regents. When I was there, one of the regents made his feelings toward democracy clear by this rhetorical query: "Does the king ask his subjects for permission to rule?"

The University of Texas was becoming more and more like an industry, and less and less like a bastion of intellectual freedom. It was turning into a commercial plant run like a factory by people whose gaze was fixed on some bottom line rather than a lofty goal. Consequently, individuals were of negligible importance, and especially insignificant were those without tenure, those who carne from a plentiful labor pool and had no power, which was the only thing that mattered to bureaucrats. They didn't have to treat powerless people fairly or pay them decently because, after all, plenty more were available and willing in a buyer's market. From all indications, the lords of Texas academia were no more concerned with justice, fairness, and decency than the most ruthless modern CEO or the bosses of the packinghouse in Upton Sinclair's *The Jungle* who let a hapless employee leave their factory as sausage.

I make these unsavory comparisons because we ought to expect more--no, we should demand more--of academia. Exploitation should not be tolerated in the ivory tower, traditionally the refuge of idealism, not crass commercialism. Campuses should be places of hope, havens of integrity and high-mindedness, not factories turning out products by callously exploiting labor--the paper graders. But exploitation is the rule, not the exception.

I last taught at Austin Community College, a plant that has grown tremendously in just a few years and, since the bureaucratic lust for terrain is boundless, plans more growth for the future. This institution, like so many others, depends upon part-time faculty to do most of the teaching, for which they are paid only 40% of what the full-time faculty would get for the same work. The average amount a part-time teacher receives for teaching one three-hour course per semester is $1,200, whereas a full-time teacher receives $3,000 *plus benefits* for the same work. Such a discrepancy unmistakably declares that the services of the part-timers are far less valuable than those of full-time faculty, yet the college employs almost ten times more adjunct faculty than regular faculty, and assigns the majority of courses to adjuncts.

The administrative hypocrisy is obvious: out of one side of its mouth the college says, "We trust your skills and abilities so much that we're assigning most of the teaching to you," and out of the other side, "We think you're not worth paying decently." Or treated decently. Dozens of us shared one small office, occupying desks like shift workers; we were hired on a semester-to-semester basis and denied medical insurance coverage or any benefits that were standard for the regular faculty; we were disdained by the administration and treated like field workers with no rights whatever. Here, for example, is a memo sent by the campus manager to the field workers:

AUSTIN COMMUNITY COLLEGE

Memorandum

To: Part-time Faculty
From· Campus Manager
Date: April 24, 1989
Re: Clearing Part-Time Offices--Begins May 19

My office will be straightening part-time faculty offices over the semester break. In order to facilitate that process and safeguard your things, please do the following:

*Remove (or discard) all papers and files from desk drawers, table tops, tops of file cabinets, etc.

*Remove all personal items (books may be left on bookshelves at your own risk!).

*Clearly mark any items which belong to you but must be left in the offices. Please label with your name and the date when you will claim the materials. (If you need a box for files or papers, check first with Duplication, then with my office).   ·

We will not touch anything inside file cabinets, but will begin clearing offices on May 19. Everything not labeled or removed as described will be tossed. Thank you for your cooperation.

The campus manager never "straightened" the offices of full-time faculty, some of which were messy and packed to the ceiling with accumulated books and papers. The part-timers, however, were subject to such treatment as a matter of course. I thought the memo--and the attitude that prompted it--outrageous, and I sent the following to the campus manager:

AUSTIN COMMUNITY COUEGE

Memorandum

To: Campus Manager
From: Part-Time Faculty
Date: May 9, 1989
Re: Clearing Part-Time Offices

This office finds your memo offensive, especially its imperious and arrogant tone (material will be "tossed," etc.). Apparently it is a warning and not a request for "cooperation."

"Straightening the office" is one thing; emptying the desk drawers and destroying people's property or teaching materials is another.

What your message clearly says is that instructors are not permitted to keep materials in the desks from semester to semester--certainly not without your approval. What are the drawers FOR? Obviously we don't have enough filing cabinets or space to begin with, and now you want to make the drawers unusable. Why are you taking it upon yourself to police the desk drawers? What does this action have to do with proper administration? Why are you impinging on the little space we have, which is sorely inadequate?

An administration that cares about its part-time faculty would be trying to find ways to help, not to hinder. But, of course, you know that.

We get your message loud and clear.

I saw no mention of my memo in any of the bulletins, newsletters, or other information streams coming from the manager's office. But since I knew that sending the memo was like dropping it into an administrative black hole, I composed a letter which I sent to five students:

September 1, 1989

Dear _____

I regret to inform you that I am unable to return your final literature paper, which was among a few others that I put in the desk I was using during the spring semester. While I was on vacation, the campus manager "tossed" the office (her term) and destroyed the contents of the desks under the ruse of "straightening the office." Although we who work at ACC are accustomed to administrative beadledom, even I was surprised by such a callous act--an act that violates more than one principle of education, not to mention common courtesy and human decency.

I'm very sorry that your work was thrown away, and I want you to know that I respect your efforts and that I would never have treated anything you submitted to me in such a cavalier fashion. I apologize because you deserve an apology and an explanation, neither of which are you likely to get from the person who destroyed your work.

Regretfully,

Ben Satterfield

cc: Campus dean
    Humanities chairperson

The dean was much displeased that a field hand would assert himself (and I expect embarrassed at the exposure). The response I got was prompt:

AUSTIN COMMUNITY COUEGE

Memorandum

To: Ben Satterfield
From: Steve Kinslow
Date: September 6, 1989
Re: Letters to Students

Ben, it was with great disappointment that I read the letter you sent to five students whose papers were thrown away by the Campus Manager when she cleaned the part-time faculty office.

The fact that papers were thrown away is one issue. Clearly, you are very angry about that and equally clear is the fact that you misinterpreted the reasons why the Campus Manager cleared the part-time faculty offices. It might interest you to know that a number of part-time faculty thanked her for her actions because many people were having difficulty finding adequate desk, shelf, and file space in the over-crowded part-time faculty offices. A "Spring Cleaning" of offices which are utilized by many individuals each semester--one during the thineen years I have been on this campus--is not worthy of the emotionalism displayed on your part. Also, your letter made no attempt to explain to students that instructors were given advance notice that the general cleaning was about to take place, or that notices were posted by the office door (copy attached). Whether or not you agree with the clean-up or how it was communicated, you do bear some responsibility for having the materials thrown away. I received one anonymous memo critical of the Campus Manager's actions, and one caustic note was taped to the wall of the office you shared. In a Campus Update I attempted to clarify for the author(s) of those notes that the action had taken place only to make offices more serviceable to all the inhabitants of them.

The other issue is more perplexing to me. Specifically, find your conduct, in regard to the letters, to be very unprofessional. Whether or not the Campus Manager is the unscrupulous, callous individual you portrayed (and judging from the feedback I receive from many instructors, they would disagree with you) is not the issue. What is an issue with me is that you thought it acceptable to present as negative an image of not only the Campus Manager but of ACC in general. Your letter evidences the same insensitivity and maliciousness of which you indict the Campus Manager. Moreover, this kind of "sniping" seems rather immature. Why have you not come to either the Campus Manager, the Division Chairperson, or me to discuss your anger and concern about these lost papers? Why would you not ask the Campus Manager if she cared to explain the incident to the students? Or me?

Ben, you do not have the market cornered on respect for students and their work, or reverence for the written word. The self-serving and vindictive nature of your *letter may indicate more to former students than you would prefer. Other than highlighting your frustration and unhappiness, nothing positive results from your letter. It doesn't reverse the regrettable loss of the papers;* it *doesn't enhance students' opinion of you or of this campus/college. What did you accomplish?*

Please make an appointment to meet with me. I am interested in *discussing this with you, as well as other concerns you may have about teaching here.*

I met with the dean, a little man with a prematurely gray beard and a high-pitched nasal voice that commanded no authority, in his office--and a nice office it was, too, recently remodeled and very comfortable. In person, the dean was more pleasant than his memo might indicate (perhaps because of his slight stature and weak voice, he found it impossible to be intimidating except in writing). With a perfectly straight face he claimed that the purpose of the office "straightening" was to help the part-time faculty, since the office was crowded with material, some of which had been left by former teachers. Knowing how cramped we were, he was, he assured me, merely trying to create more space for us.

I asked why one of the smaller classrooms could not be converted into an additional office to help relieve the overcrowding, at times so bad that conferring with students was impossible; many teachers talked to their students in the halls or took them outside if weather permitted. I was wasting my breath. Giving up a classroom would mean forfeiting the income from twenty or thirty classes a semester, and the college often allowed enrollment to exceed set limits as things were, packing rooms sometimes beyond capacity and adding to the teachers' burdens.   When I wondered why administrative "concern" expressed itself negatively--by destroying property--rather than positively, he appeared bewildered. Apparently, the idea of doing something positive was totally alien to him and he was lost, wanting an example. I suggested that he could add another filing cabinet to the office, and he said, "I never thought of that." I'm sure he was being truthful. (He did furnish the office with an additional filing cabinet shortly thereafter.)

   For the most part, the dean seemed sincere and genuine, so disarming that I left his office feeling good about the encounter. Management skills at work.

   This dean, who was the best of the various deans spread over several campuses, never perceived his own hypocrisy and consequently was unable to understand why people might be discontented or why everyone didn't see things they way he saw them.   Once, when the Part-Time Faculty Association, an organization created to address problems the dean ignored, criticized the college for purchasing an office building while spurning the needs of its adjunct faculty (a lack of funds was the alleged reason), he responded by labeling the criticism inappropriate and explaining that ACC "got a good deal" on the building.   The college also "got a good deal" on its part-time faculty, a fact that went unmentioned.   A good business deal is self-justifying, regardless.

Because I was convinced the dean was an administrative puppet who had no interest in helping the part-time faculty, I tried to avoid contact with him. Over the years, though, necessity forced me to send him a few memos, half of which he did not deign to answer, despite his claim that he would respond and do so promptly. So much for his assurances. When pressed on a legitimate issue, he often did nothing, and his disregard caused additional problems for the teaching staff since he could not be relied on for anything except hot air. Neglect is a kick to one's spirit that is more bruising than words: the understood message is, "You're not worth answering."

My gorge was filled. After being repeatedly shamed by my second-class status, I sent the following:

AUSTIN COMMUNITY COLLEGE

Memorandum
To: *Steve Kinslow*
From: *Ben Satterfield*
Date: *September 4, 1992*
Re: *Office access*

Will you tell me why I am not allowed to have a key to Room 300 (the pan-time instructors' office)?

For three semesters running, I submitted a key request form, only to discover--finally--that people in the Security Office will not issue a key to Room 300.

I have been locked out of this office at least half a dozen times, most recently night before last. Not having a key to Room 300 has proven inconvenient (to say the least) and, on one occasion, embarrassing, as my entire class had to stand in the hall and wait until I could find someone to let me into the office (that experience was almost humiliating).

Perhaps being denied a key to the office is just another indignity that I'm expected to suffer, but I see no reason for it.

A diplomat would doubtless have tempered the final paragraph, but it expressed my sentiments precisely, and, as I said, my gorge was full. Evidently, so was the dean's.

AUSTIN COMMUNITY COLLEGE

Memorandum

To: Ben Satterfield
From: Steve Kinslow
Date: September 8, 1992
Re: Office Access

I've attached your September 4 memo and request that you read it again. It's a good example of exaggerating something out of proportion to its significance, and it's a tad melodramatic. Obviously you were angry when you wrote it, but then you seem to almost always be angry on this campus. Despite your vitriol, we do not conspire to make you "suffer" nor to heap one "indignity" after another upon you.

Neither I, the Campus Manager, or the Division Chairperson deny office keys to part-time faculty. In checking with the Security Office I learned that they were not issuing keys to Room 300 because it is on schedule to be unlocked throughout the day. It is apparent, however, that on a few occasions someone locked it when making building rounds--usually late in the evening or on Fridays after classes ended. We have clarified for Security that they may not deny any key requests; all requests they question will be forwarded to me for review and final action. Security staff made a mistake, and they regret it. As soon as we knew about it we corrected it. There was no conspiracy to denigrate your worth as an instructor or as a human being; no one plots to make teaching inconvenient and unpleasant for you. One wonders why you would choose to be resentful of this for three semesters without requesting that either the Division Chairperson or I check into it and respond to you. It's really that simple, Ben--if something occurs that distresses you, let your supervisor know about it when it occurs instead of feeling and acting resentful and petulant long afterwards. Not only is that a more professional thing to do, it's also more mature. It is my opinion that you prefer to look for "slights" from staff on this campus, and that you prefer to feel martyred in coping with occasional problems that occur rather than constructively trying to work them out and giving people the benefit of the doubt that most have good intentions even when they make mistakes. I also believe that it is human nature for individuals to respond in the same manner in which they are approached, and that minor situations (such as the key issue) can remain unresolved when staff feel that they were approached in less than a congenial manner or spirit. I don't know anyone on this campus who is perfect, Ben. It may be that you should consider teaching at another ACC campus (or another institution) since your behavior consistently indicates unhappiness here.

A key is enclosed. Is there anything else we can do for you this semester?

AUSTIN COMMUNITY COLLEGE

Memorandum

To:	*Steven Kinslow*
From:	*Ben Satterfield*
Date:	*September 9, 1992*
Re:	*Key (and communication)*

Thank you for your promptness in responding to my memo--and double thanks for securing a key for my use. I appreciate your help.

Of course you believe it appropriate to respond emotionally to my memo, which I wrote less in anger than in frustration, but for you to say that I "seem to almost always be angry on this campus" is a gross exaggeration (ask anyone who knows me). In truth, your analysis of my behavior (and character) is off the mark, just as is your assumption that I chose to be resentful for three semesters (actually four) rather than approach the Division Chairperson or you. I did ask the Chairperson about this matter last year, and he assured me that he "signed the form and sent it" to your office. Since the Security people never had the form when I inquired, I resubmitted key request forms--and not in anger, petulance, or resentment--each semester. Only this year did I learn that the Security Office would not issue keys to Room 300 (apparently all my request forms were discarded upon receipt, but I have no way of knowing). During the break last month, I came to campus one day, planning to do some paperwork to get a jump on the fall semester, but the office was locked. Rather than tromp up and down the stairs seeking one of the Security people, who are not always cordial, I just left. Once before, when I approached one of the men (who was making building rounds at the time) and told him that I was locked out of my office and asked--nicely, I assure you--if he would open it, he inquired, "Which one?" When I told him 300, he said, "I'll be there in a while." I don't propose to read minds, but it seems evident that once he learned I wanted to get into the part-time faculty office, he saw no need for alacrity or attention, much less courtesy, and I had to wait in the hall until he deigned to let me in. That qualifies as an indignity, and if you think I'm being melodramatic or immature, consider for a moment how you might feel if treated this way.

I have been, as I said, locked out at least half a dozen times, but you state that "on a few occasions someone locked" the room and thereby imply that I was not being truthful. You call my complaint "a good example of exaggerating something out of proportion to its significance," but show no sensitivity to my "long-suffering" in this matter. I didn't just blow up; after four semesters, I reached the end of my rope. I simply could not understand why I was denied a key. I made no mention of nor did I imply any "conspiracy"; I am not paranoid--but I am sensitive (perhaps as sensitive as you). I do not think that you or the Division chairperson or the campus manager or anyone else conspires to make me suffer, and any suggestion of conspiracy was uncalled for, and, from my point of view, unprofessional.

You seem to think that if I perceive the least little slight I fire off a memo to you, but such is not the case. I communicate with you only as a last resort. I wish that you would not assume the worst about me and I also wish that you would read my memos with more care. I do not exaggerate and I do not lie, and I do not need to be "talked down to" or told the obvious.

To end on a positive note, I assert that a very real problem existed with the Security Office, and as a result of my memo, the problem was brought to your attention and rectified. Good. It certainly was high time, and I think I was more than tolerant.

The dean chose not to reply. Faced with a choice of responding to me in any fashion or ignoring me altogether, he opted for the latter; neglect is an effective management tactic that helps keep people down.

I left at the end of the semester.

THE ADJUNCT

Carolyn Foster Segal

Well, as I told my friend Pete,
it's a hell of a career
choice, teaching
the comma
to a hostile audience
for a very small fee,
but I'm keeping
my resume alive.   "So what

is the meaning of
meaning?" I asked my students,
while listening to Bach's
Brandenburg Concerto #5
in my head.
"Exactly," I shouted
over the music
when nobody answered.

Here is today's lecture:
imagination is out.
Experience is in. I am in
trouble, not having had
a direct experience for at
least a decade, After all,
I'm an adjunct.
You may want to take

certified notes
from someone with tenure.

Who isn't here? Just
call out your uame.
This morning
we're deconstructiug
Thoreau's cabin.
In the words of Gertrude Stein,
"What is a nail?"

THE WOMAN WHO GRADES THEMES

Carolyn Foster Segal

(after Diane Wakoski's "Man Who Paints
   Mountains")

You are cut off
like Kafka. You think of the snowy dissertation,
look at the theme in your hand.
Your pencil mark, with skill, glides into parallel structure
but will anyone ever know what you mean by it?

You are cut off
like Dickinson. Each pencil mark grows smaller,
more precise
but you have given up all hope of communication
and scarcely speak.

Ellipsis after ellipsis
fills your work. And they say, "Oh, yes,
she is the woman who grades themes."

In a slightly different form, this poem originally appeared
in The PCTE Bulletin

THE DEATH OF THE PH.D: A RANT

David Starkey

Dan Quayle couldn't do it. Jesse Helms couldn't do
it. They're too stupid. They have insufficient
post-graduate experience. We did it to ourselves. Or,
rather, our shadow senior "selves" did it to us. The
institutionalization of non-tenured writing faculty has
made the Ph.D. in English superfluous. The Doctor of
Philosophy, wan Narcissus, lovesick for itself, has
committed suicide. Only Echo remains, and that Echo
is us, the writing staff--adjuncts and part-timers,
graduate students and permanent instructors--transformed
for far too long from solid body into an ineffectual,
moaning voice.

But that voice is reassembling itself, nucleotide by
nucleotide, into torsos like this anthology. Frankenstein's
monster shakes his head, opens his eyes, and says, "I no
longer need the doctor." Understand: i f the university
administration is going to maintain English Departments
as places where, first and foremost, writing is taught,
then we must acknowledge, must thrive on this change.
Like dogs who have been kicked once too often, we are
biting back, even if it means an irrevocable trip to the
pound.

*

The Ph.D. may once have been the union card for
entry into Departments of Literature. Now it is a union
card for the unemployment line.

So what do we do with literature courses and departments? *Gone.*

Ah, I hear you out there protesting wildly, you who have spent four, seven, ten years taking classes, passing comps, endlessly revising your dissertations to suit the whims of some antiquated lunatic who received his degree from Hooterville State and fell into a job in the 1960s when they were handing out tenured professorships to anyone who could spell "Jack Keats." And now that you have run the gauntlet, you want the reward. You, too, want to sit back in your office and unbend paper clips, lounge in fine hotels three times a semester, teach 2-1 with sabbaticals every other year. Of course you do! But you keep scanning the *Job List* and the *Chronicle* only to find all the positions in the sweet research universities of the liberal north vanishing before your eyes. Professor Briar Patches, you are pure fantasy! Week-by-week it becomes more evident that the employment of the future is a year-to-year contract, 7-8 with ten hours a week of service in a community college in south central Georgia: "Yawl understand that yawl is lucky to have any job--period."

*

Again, if we have been forced out of the promised land, let us go, not gracefully, but with vengeful purpose to a new home.

"Why do we have to read this poem?" the lethargic sophomores ask when we are allowed to teach a survey course, and our answers are myriad and ingenious. Primarily, though, it is because we ourselves love poetry. We have devoted our beings to it. But fear not: poetry will survive without literature departments. How grand it is, the Faculty of Literature. They tolerate us, but they don't really need us. They drink with us after hours, but when we want to teach their classes . . . . The truth is, of course, that we don't need them at all.

Be gone, de facto conservatives, you who vote Democratic but stand by sipping brandy as your own kind are herded into the slaughterhouse and butchered before your eyes!

I see this: I see literature classes scaled back to a few surveys taught by everyone. In a small college in Georgia there is absolutely no need for, let us say, a medievalist. Farm boy, farm girl, I give you a choice. Do you want to learn to write a sentence as strong and lean as your pappy's arms, or will you have Sir Orfeo instead. You cannot have both. You are poor and hurried and harried. Choose wisely.

Oh, my colleagues, but I hear you saying that in a small college in Georgia there is more need for a medievalist than anywhere else. We are Guardians of the Humanities. And are we to condemn these young people to everlasting Crackerdom simply because of where they were born? If we don't keep literature alive in the rural South, in the cauldron of ignorance, the indifference of the populace will soon spread everywhere. Jesse Helms will make sure of that.

Yet how sad, how naive that argument is. The young man whose crucial spiritual experience came when his father hung the testicles of his first deer around his neck, the young woman who spends hours each morning to freeze her bangs into the drama of an ocean wave, they need no cuckoo to tell them when "sumer is icumen in."

*

I look around at my colleagues and see M.A.s teaching with more fluency than Ph.D.s. The Masters spend many hours   preparing, conferencing, and grading.   Like their Ph.D. companions, they present papers at conferences and are passionate about their work. But the Doctors have an unconquerable handicap. All the while they are workshopping a comparison and contrast essay, they are groaning, inwardly and outwardly, that they cannot discuss intricate problems of 17th century British economic theory with their freshmen. The freshmen just don't get it. No, they don't! And the Doctors end up making five thousand dollars a year more for doing less work: not because they are by nature or by inclination worse teachers--these people are my friends--but simply because they have been brainwashed into thinking that teaching writing is not worthwhile. And why shouldn't they, when they see the rewards that it brings those devoted to it?

*

Meanwhile, one or three or five years later, everyone's contract expires. Everyone is out on her ass looking for   another job.   The great exodus to Macon begins.

Ph.D.s in Rhetoric and Composition? Well, they are a gesture in the right direction, but that gesture is too little too late.   Already the programs are mired in internal politics, the theories are increasingly abstruse, decreasingly applicable to the day-to-day life of a practicing instructor.

The Master of Arts is, therefore, the new final degree. Give me an intelligent hard-working person willing to spend two years teaching composition and studying the teaching of writing, and I will give you someone who can do a job superior to that of any nascent Ivy League Professor.

Yes, I know, you think I am a dreamer. Clearly, there will continue to be Doctors of Philosophy. Harvard and Yale aren't likely to discontinue their programs. Scholars, more vain and more impotent than ever, will huddle in special collections libraries hidden like bunkers in the great cities of America. They will keep the flames of Grimald and Shenstone and St. John Gogarty alive. But the public will rightfully go on ignoring them, and finally the rest of us in the new Departments of Writing can begin ignoring them, too.

When the Ph.D. effectively breathes its last, there will be no justification for paying brilliant researchers more than brilliant teachers, or for paying one group of peons more than another. Seniority and effectiveness will count for everything. The permanent instructor with an M.A. who has been teaching comp for twenty years and has a windowless office in the basement will not receive one-third the salary of her new colleagues, the twenty-eight-year-old assistant professor from Berkeley. The lion and the lamb will lie down together at last.

*

There is a great deal to be said for the Ph.D. in English. Right now you are no doubt saying it yourselves. But, in the end, there is simply not enough. The Ph.D. makes possible--no, makes necessary-- the exploitation of writing faculty. As long as the important work we do is only considered a stepping stone to something more valuable, we will continue to be trampled on.

Come, sisters and brothers, even if you are already burdened with an excess of philosophy. Our vocations are at stake.

The degree is terminal. For God's sake, let's put it out of its misery.

NO PAY FOR SICK DAYS

Julia Stein

Third week my right ear is clogged up,
pain radiates out,
could barely hear my students
talk in English so quietly as they slowly
tread their way into a new language,
Paid by the hour, nothing for sick days,
I drag my tired self to work all week.
Thursday, exhausted, ear aches, in my kitchen
water's all over the floor, call plumber,
on my hands and knees, sop up water with towels.
The plumber came, my ear cleared up by Monday
I was in front of the class--the worst hill climbed,
it was downhill the rest of the semester.

CHEAP BATTERIES

Julia Stein

I never complained about the huge class,
the ghastly schedule given me, a new part-time college
instructor. At least the department chairman promised
me I can choose the books for my class until

the ex-chairperson of the department
told me I can't have the books I want.
Two days later on the stairs she ordered me
to take her handouts. I shook my head "no."

She told me I'm replaceable. "It's easy to hire
someone else to teach your class." Where I work
teachers are cheap batteries, plug one in, when
it burns out, unplug it, plug a new one in.

Originally published in Pearl

WAITING FOR THE EARTHQUAKE

Julia Stein

What's the price of my life?
Not much in this school system.
My South Central LA classroom sits
right on top of the earthquake fault.
Four stories of classrooms have a sign on front,
"You enter this building at your own risk."

I hated the rich people who refused to raise
their property taxes so we can have
safe buildings, abandoning us on the fault,
I returned to teach after the riots
a mile from Florence and Normandy Avenues,
the heart of the burning in Los Angeles,

heard my summer school class cut,
then I get a class, up and down this
see-saw never quits waiting for the
next earthquake, riot or cut-backs,
hanging on for dear life or I'll
fall off down into the scrap heap.

Pain runs up my back. Can't stand up
straight. Walk very slowly.
My first backache. Go to sleep.
Wake up bed shaking oh no an earthquake.
I'm too weak to get out of bed, just feel
my back aching, the earth shaking.

Originally published in Pearl

GRAMMAR IN SOUTH CENTRAL
LOS ANGELES

Julia Stein

Smoke chokes the city's sky Thursday
Buildings in flames all around me in noose of fire.
The radio says all schools closed no teaching.
On my day off I see broken glass and empty shelves
of the looted clothing store five blocks away,
burnt timbers smoldering on Pico Boulevard,
two National Guard in front of the supermarket.
Monday I return to teach in South Central
snipers are still shooting at the National Guard.
I drive down LaBrea Avenue, see black rubble--
what's left of a bank and a shoe store.

Fifteen students sit quietly on the steps of my bungalow.
Luis, a Mexican, wears black sunglasses in class.
He was beaten up driving his taxi in Long Beach.
Maria from El Salvador has nightmares.
She lives in the middle of the riot zone.
It effects her nerves and her eyes.
I hope she doesn't go blind.
All the groceries stores in Juan's neighborhood burned.
We talk a few minutes more, then
I write the new lesson on the chalkboard:
yes, I believe
verbs, writing and reason will lead us
to a new grammar of hope.

Originally published in Pearl

TIRED OF WAITING

Julia Stein

Waiting for the janitors to come turn on the heat in the
    classroom in South Central Los Angeles,
waiting for them to build us a safe classroom,
    off the earthquake fault,
    with a clock in the wall,
waiting for them to fix the tile in the basement ceiling,
waiting for enough chairs,
waiting for the keys to the classroom,
waiting for the books to arrive,
waiting for the lights to be turned on at night near the
    classrooms,
eighty part-time teachers waiting in line to apply for one
    full-time teaching job,
before the riots we were patiently
waiting.

After the riots in Los Angeles
    when all the politicians came to South Central
    stood in front of the burned out buildings
    had their photos taken
    making promises,
the President came
the Governor came
the Mayor came
the State Assemblymen came
the State Senators came
we read the newspapers each morning kept waiting
patiently.

In May we heard all our summer school classes cut
    I lost my summer job,
then we had half the summer classes put back,
    I got my job back,
in the middle of the summer we heard teachers cut for fall,
    not me this time,
in the fall we heard 50% cuts of classes,
    I lost my job,
seventy students went to the Board of Trustees,
    asked for their classes back,
    I got my job back,
    the instructor as human yo-yo,
in January we heard the Governor wants to cut our jobs again,
    11% cut,
    will my job get bulldozed away again?
I'm tired of waiting,
no, I'm not patient,
anymore,
I want
the promises kept,
now.

TEACHING IN THE '90s

Julia Stein

Goodbye, goodbye sweet students
when you didn't have chairs you stand up writing your lessons,
I'm ordered to only teach 40,
53 are here at my City College class, I'm
sorry, five have to leave,
they bulldozed your classes to smithereens.

At the end of the semester
you gave me a fine gift, a warm black sweater,
good bye, sweet students,
I have to go,
can't live on this tiny wage,
hopefully we'll see each other, one day, I
have a class photo one of you took, sweet
students I treasure it.

8:00 in the morning, Southwest Junior College, in
South Central Los Angeles
the medical students call it the war zone,
emergency rooms full of young men with gunshot wounds
from gang shootings.
Temperature near freezing.
Bundled up in my black sweater in the classroom.
All my students want this cold morning is
the heater to work,
sweet students, I've complained five times,
they're having a Gulf war this semester,

no money to fix the heat,
the tile ceiling in the hall is falling down,
more empty holes than ceiling,
no money to fix the tiles.

Sweet students,
we'll try for a bond measure on the ballot
if it passes
we'll build a nursing school,
and build a real bookstore
where you walk up and down the aisles to actually
hold the book in your hand
well, the taxpayers voted it down,
no money for a bookstores this year,
no nursing building,
no heat for the classroom,
no money to fix the tile ceiling.

I'll tell you I want:
my classroom always to have heat sizzling through the vents;
my students to have enough chairs all semester
so we can all sit down;
a new nursing school full of students in labs,
all the cut classes back like phoenixes reborn;
yes, I want it all, a wooden desk by a window
in a cubicle office,
with a swivel metal chair where I can sit down
surrounded by phoenixes.

Originally published in Pearl. *The recorded version is
on the CD* DisClosure *(New Alliance Records)*

THE PART-TIME TEACHER DOES NOT LIKE HER CONTRACT

Judy Wells

The part-time teacher is asked to sign a contract which says she will give up her course to a full-time faculty member if he or she needs it. Every time she reaches that section, she balks. No, I will not give up my course to a full-time faculty member, she says. Absolutely not. I won't. This has never happened. Still, the part-time teacher does not want to sign her contract. "Thanks for your cooperation," says the contract.

The part-time teacher wonders whether electricians or grape pickers would sign a contract signing away their jobs. She wonders why hundreds of part-time teachers sitting at home at their desks, pens poised above their contracts, do not refuse to sign on the dotted line. She wonders whether she ought to call in the California Self-Esteem Task Force and ask them what is wrong.

Originally published in The Part-Time Teacher *(Rainy Day Women Press, 1991)*

THE PART-TIME TEACHER WANTS TO START A UNION

Judy Wells

The part-time teacher goes to a meeting whose subject is IMPROVING SUPPORT FOR PART-TIME TEACHERS. The administrator spends the first 15 minutes telling the part-time teachers about the chain of command at the college. He says the President is God. "Goddess," corrects the speech teacher. The President is a woman.

Next, part-time teachers complain about not being able to xerox 30 copies of handouts for their students. They are only allowed 20 copies for 30 students. The administrator adjusts his rimless glasses, looks handsome and suave, and grants them 10 more copies.

The part-time teacher meditates on the memo she has already sent the administrator. "Ten extra copies are nice, but need I remind you that it would be very supportive of you to offer us health insurance and eligibility for unemployment, extra pay for office hours, a real contract, and a guaranteed key to the ladies' room?" He promises parking permits and posters, bandaids for cancer.

Orginally published in The Part-Time Teacher *(Rainy Day Women Press, 1991)*

THE PART-TIME TEACHER MEETS A
FELLOW TRAVELER

Judy Wells

The part-time teacher applies to teach THE GREAT BOOKS at a Catholic college. She is asked to observe the class of "one of the finest instructors of the course." She calls him on the phone. The class is off campus in the basement of a hospital 20 miles from their homes, across a bridge. They decide to go together, and the instructor tells her, "I have a van with no heat, so if you want heat, we'd better take your car." The part-time teacher knows right away he is poor. But her car is 15 years old, and she too wants to conserve it, so she says, "I don't mind bundling up."

In his van, she finds out he has degrees in all kinds of things from all kinds of places. He wrote his dissertation in Germany in German and had it published. He also has a theological degree and used to be a poet when he had more time. He is writing a novel but he needs more time. The part-time teacher asks him whether he is trying to piece it all together with part-time teaching. Yes, he says. He has a class on Marx in San Francisco with only four students. How much does it pay? she inquires. $400, he sighs, only $100 a head, and does she know anyone who's interested in dialectical materialism? No, she confesses, but would he like to take a class in creative writing; she needs more students. He said he'd like to, but he doesn't have the time. He is teaching another course on rituals for the dead.

Do you meet many Ph.D.'s in your travels who are part-time teachers? she inquires. Yes, he confides. They are all at the Catholic college. He tears down the freeway on the rainy night like a man who knows his destiny is driving, and he's driving for his life and so is she.

Originally published in The Part-Time Teacher *(Rainy Day Women Press, 1991)*

CONTRIBUTOR PROFILES

JEAN ANDERSON's collection, *In Extremis and Other Alaskan Stories,* was nominated tor the annual Sue Kaufman Award for first fiction given by the American Academy of Arts and Letters. One story in the collection received a PEN Syndicated Fiction selection. Anderson is co-editor of the regional anthology *Inroads: Alaska's 27 Fellowship Writers.* She has lived in Fairbanks since 1966 and has taught on and off at the University of Alaska since 1980, recently as a visiting assistant professor in 1990-91. She is currently at work on a collection of Siberian and Alaskan stories with the working title, *Bird's Milk.*

KAT SNIDER BLACKBIRD is a poet, performance artist, and part-time creative writing teacher at Kent State University. Kent State Press published *White Sustenance,* her new book, in December of 1993. Her verse has also appeared in *The New York Quarterly, The Midwest Quarterly Journal for Contemporary Thought, New Kent Quarterly,* and other publications. She is the winner of Kent State's Wick Poetry Prize, the Lakeland Poetry Prize, and three time winner of the Dubois Award. Blackbird has been asked to perform and read her work by the James Wright Poetry Festival, the Columbus Arts Festival, the Northern Michigan Bonfire Festival of Oral Tradition, The Forest Gathering of Poets, the C.G. Jung Educational Center of Cleveland, and elsewhere. She also uses poetry in nursing homes for healing, and conducts poetry workshops for elementary and high school students.

CAYLE is a Philadelphia poet who has worked as an underpaid actor, theater technician, cook, census taker, carpenter, instructor for the developmentally disabled, and university writing teacher. Cayle staged a verse play in Bethlehem and organized radio poetry readings in Allentown, where he also coordinated a poetry series funded by the Pennsylvania Arts Council. He has won an Allen Ginsberg Award for his poetry as well as a Special Merit Award from *Poet* magazine. His work has appeared in *The American Poetry Review, Philadelphia Poets, Pacific Review, Widener Review,* and elsewhere.

DAVID EHRENFELD, an outspoken critic of corruption in the modern American university, is the founding editor of *Conservation Biology,* author of *Beginning Again: People and Nature in the New Millennium* (Oxford, 1993), *The Arrogance of Humanism* (Oxford, 1978, 1981), and coauthor, with C.K. Mark, of *The Chameleon Variant* (Dial, 1980), a science fiction novel. Ehrenfeld teaches undergraduate and graduate courses in ecology at Rutgers University.

BARRY GREER taught creative, environmental, and professional writing for ten years at the University of Oregon and Oregon State University. He is the author of *Black Mountain,* a novel (FreeSolo Press), and has a short story in the 1993 Pig Iron Press anthology. His fiction, essays, articles, and commentary have appeared in *New Republic, High Plains Literary Review, Dog River Review, Appalachia, Orion Nature Quarterly, Snowy Egret, Buzzworm,* and elsewhere. Greer is a member of the National Writers Union.

RICHARD HILL's latest novels are *Shoot the Piper* (St. Martin's, 1994) and *Riding Solo with the Golden Horde* (University of Georgia Press, 1994). He's the author of twelve other books, including ten novels and a short story collection. His work has appeared in *Harper's, Esquire, Omni, Playboy, The New York Times Book Review, Rolling Stone, Utne Reader, Witness, Kenyon Review,* the Pig Iron Press anthology and other publications. Hill won an O. Hemy Prize, an NEA Fellowship, a PEN/Algren citation, has been cited in *Notable Essays,* was a finalist for a Stegner Fellowship, was the first Raymond Chandler Fulbright scholar to Oxford, and he received a fiction award from the Florida Fine Arts Council. He's has been a fellow at Ragsdale, Yaddo, the MacDowell Colony, Virginia Center for the Creative Arts, and elsewhere. And he's been a migrant university instructor for 28 years, most recently teaching at the University of North Carolina.

MARK HILLRINGHOUSE teaches French and creative writing at Passaic County College in New Jersey. He served as poetry director for the William Carlos Williams Center for the Arts, and has worked as an editor for *The New York Arts Journal* and *The American Book Review.* He's now an associate editor of *joe soap's canoe,* a British poetry journal. Hillringhouse was nominated for a Pushcart Prize and won two fellowships in poetry from the New Jersey State Council on the Arts. He also conducts poetry workshops for the Geraldine R. Dodge Foundation's Poets-in-the-Schools Program. His work has appeared in the *New York Times, American Poetry, Columbia, Passages North, American Poetry Review,* and in *Bluestones and Salt Hay,* an anthology of New Jersey Poets (Rutgers UP).

CHARLES HOOD quit a Ph.D. program to study ethnopoetics on a Fulbright to New Guinea, and from there was a freeway flyer for many years before settling in at Antelope Valley College, where he teaches developmental composition, literature, and creative writing. His 1990 poetry book, *Red Sky, Red Water* follows John Wesley Powell's 1869 descent of the Colorado River. At present he's working on two book projects, one about World War II and the other the rain forests of Costa Rica. He would welcome either an NEA grant or a Message From Above in order to complete either one.

MARIA THERESA MAGGI is a temporary lecturer of composition and creative writing at the University of Idaho. She's also lectured at the University of California and taught in the California Poets in the Schools program. Her poetry and reviews have appeared in *The Alaska Quarterly Review, The Florida Review, Black Warrior Review, Prairie Schooner,* and *Magill's Literary Annual,* and her work was nominated in 1992 for a Pushcart Prize.

CHRISTINA MCVAY was a Fulbright Scholar at the University of Bonn and is now a part-time literature and writing teacher at Kent State University in the English Department and in the Pan-African Studies Department, where she serves as director of the Communication Skills Division. She also teaches elementary and intermediate courses in the German Department. She edits and publishes *Pro-fess-ing,* a biweekly newsletter for part-timers read on several northern Ohio campuses, was a co-president of the Ohio Adjunct Faculty Association, and serves on the national AAUP committee on adjuncts. McVay was the first part-time Kent State instructor to teach an honors colloquium, and she is now lobbying hard to gain faculty senate representation for part-timers as official recognition of their professional contribution to Kent State.

NAOMI RACHEL has published poems and essays in more than 200 quarterlies, including *North American Review, Massachusetts Review, Wisconsin Review, Kansas Quarterly, Berkeley Poetry Review, Wild Earth,* and others. Two anthologies, *Contemporary California Poets* and *Women Poets,* have included her work. In 1993 Senex Press of San Francisco published her chapbook, *The Temptation of Extinction* and she received a Nimrod Award from the Tulsa Arts and Humanities Council. Rachel teaches creative and environmental writing at the University of Colorado and teaches as a Poet in the Schools.

A.L. REILLY is a part-time college writing instructor and freelance writer with publications in ·*Outside, Chicago Tribune,* and elsewhere. She also works in corporate and documentary film. Reilly co-wrote a television pilot with Georges Collinet, host of *Afro-Pop World Wide,* a National Public Radio program. In addition she co-designed several exhibits and museums, including the Lexington Children's Museum in Kentucky. Her work has received recognition with two Spectra Awards from the International Association of Business Communicators, a National Council of Foundations Award, a Women in Communications Award, and a Chicago Film Festival Award.

MARY ROHRER-DANN has worn both adjunct and full-time instructor hats and has taught a variety of writing courses. She currently teaches fiction and advanced composition part-time at Penn State. She loves teaching, but the lack of professional development and advancement opportunities, job security, and respect from her employer for her services, are getting old. Fast. Rohrer-Dann's stories have appeared in *Cimmaron Review, Sites International, Kestrel,* and other literary magazines.

BEN SATTERFIELD taught at the University of Texas and at Austin Community College, but he now devotes his time to writing. Satterfield's fiction, poetry, drama, reviews, commentary, and criticism have appeared in commercial, literary, and academic publications, including *Studies in American Fiction, Southwest Review, Oxford Magazine, San Jose Studies, Ball State University Forum, High Plains Literary Review,* and elsewhere. A novel, *Junkman,* is forthcoming.

CAROLYN FOSTER SEGAL is an adjunct professor of English at Lehigh University in Bethlehem, Pennsylvania. She teaches freshman English, upper level and graduate courses in expository writing, creative writing, and American literature--all for a very small fee. She reads 1000 pages of drafts, papers, and revisions each semester, and has found many parallels between academia and the pickle factory where she worked one summer. Her poems, essays, and short stories have appeared in more than fifty magazines and academic journals, including *Nebraska English Journal, Pennsylvania English, Buffalo Spree,* and *Phoebe.*

ALBERT SHANKER, president of the 800,000 member American Federation of Teachers since 1974, has been a leading voice on public education policy from the White House to the National Press Club to the Economic Club of Chicago and the Fortune 500 Business Roundtable. He is an active member of the A. Philip Randolph Institute, the AFL-CIO Executive Committee, the Trilateral Commission, the Jewish Labor Committee, the National Academy of Education, the National Board for Professional Standards, and other organizations. He serves on the advisory board of the Yale School of Management and the advisory council of the Princeton University Department of Sociology. He taught at Hunter College and the Harvard Graduate School of Education, and was scholar-in-residence at the University of Chicago, Claremont College, and UCLA. Columbia University Teachers College awarded him a distinguished service medal for his lifelong dedication to improving the working conditions of teachers.

DAVID STARKEY is in his fourth year as a temporary instructor at Francis Marion University, where he teaches poetry writing, literature, and composition, and served as director of the 1994 Francis Marion Writers Conference. His publications include two books, a chapbook, and poems in *Chariton Review, Cutbank, Appalachee Quarterly, Boston Literary Review, High Plains Literary Review, Oxford Magazine,* and others. "The MFA Graduate as Composition Instructor" is included in *Colors of a Different Horse,* a 1993 NCTE anthology. *Poet* magazine cited Starkey as an outstanding teacher of poetry writing. He has also received two Pushcart nominations, two American Academy of Poetry Awards, and was a semifinalist in the "Discovery"/*The Nation* Award.

JULIA STEIN has published two books of poetry: *Desert Soldiers* (California Classics) and *Under the Ladder to Heaven* (West End Press), the latter a finalist in the American Academy of Poets Whitman contest. Her work is in numerous print anthologies, including *Calling Home Working-Class Womens' Writers* (Rutgers UP), and two tape/CD albums, *Jazzspeak* and *Disclosure* (both by New Alliance Records). She has performed over two hundred readings in Paris, London, Chicago, Honolulu, Los Angeles, and San Francisco. Stein is also widely published as a book reviewer, having written for *American Book Review, LA Weekly, Village Voice, Daily News,* and elsewhere. Currently she teaches at Southwest College and UCLA and is a founding member of the Los Angeles local of the National Writers Union.

M. ELIZABETH WALLACE established herself in 1984 as a fearless critic of part-time employment practices in higher education by editing *Part-Time Employment in the Humanities: A Sourcebook for Just Policy* (MLA). "Lower Than the Low One" was published in the fall of 1988 when Wallace entered a tenure-track position at Western Oregon State College. A second essay criticizing treatment of part-timers appeared in the Sunday Portland *Oregonian,* Oregon's largest circulation newspaper. Research for both was supported by the Northwest Independent Scholars Association and the Center for the Study of Women in Society. In the fall of 1993, WOSC granted Wallace tenure.

JUDY WELLS has published four books of poetry, *I Have Berkeley, Albuquerque Winter, Jane, Jane,* and *The Calling.* Her poetry has also been included in numerous literary magazines and in four anthologies: *Been in Berkeley Too Long, In the River the Roar of a Train, Coffee Mill Anthology,* and *Coffeehouse Poetry Anthology.* "Daddy's Girl," an essay, is in *The Borzoi College Reader,* and *The Part-Time Teacher* is her prose-poem collection about her odyssey as a part-time college instructor in the San Francisco Bay Area. She has read from *Part-Time* in coffee houses, on college campuses, and on television in Berkeley and Nashville. Her newest book, *The Calling: Poems on 20th Century Women Artists* was published in 1994. She has also completed a novel, *Purgatory Hot Springs,* and an essay collection, *A Vegetarian in Ireland.* Judy Wells has taught at Contra Costa College, Vista College, UC Berkeley, and St. Mary's College.

CPSIA information can be obtained
at www.ICGtesting.com
Printed in the USA
FSHW021124231218
54658FS

9 781479 185375